MEMORIES O_

FRIARGATE STATION

First published in Great Britain by
The Breedon Books Publishing Company Limited
Breedon House, 44 Friar Gate, Derby, DE1 1DA.
1998

ISBN 1 85983 116 8

Printed and bound by Butler & Tanner Ltd., Selwood Printing
Works, Caxton Road, Frome, Somerset.

Colour separations by RPS Ltd, Leicester.

Covers printing by Lawrence-Allen Colour Printers,
Weston-super-Mare, Avon.

MEMORIES OF
FRIARGATE STATION

S U S A N   B O U R N E

The Breedon Books
Publishing Company
Derby

Acknowledgements

I am particularly indebted to Alan Rimmer, whose photographs make an important part of the book, but the following people have all made this book possible: Pete Burns, Ken Cook, Steve Higgins, John Barnes, Bryan Bourne, Mr Blundell, James and Nicholas Coker, Mr Cresswell, Rob Passey, John and Jane Tucket, Jackie Worrel, J.McAndrews, Mike Cordon, S.Harrison, Nick Hawley, Bill Worton, Les Sayers, Jack Southall, E.A.West, J.Sainsburys, Mrs F.Siddons, Mr Seaman, Mrs O'Donnell, Lynda and Sybil Ride, John Roe, Arthur Gillman, Robin Beck, Miss E.Holmes, Maurice Oakley, Phill Stryj, Mrs Wint, Alf Bousie, Jack Wallis, Percy Sims, Dick Clegg, Rosemary York, Alf Henshaw and the Local Studies Library in Iron Gate. Readers interested in further information on the subject are recommended to read Mark Higginson's *The Friargate Line*.

Dedication

To mum and dad, with all my love.

The publishers acknowledge that the correct spelling of the thoroughfare is Friar Gate. However in the interest of consistency for this book the station spelling of Friargate has been used.

Introduction

FRIARGATE STATION closed to passengers on 6 September 1964, but the last train ran at 10.10pm on Saturday, 5 September. It closed amidst almost as much opposition as when it opened over 80 years before. According to British Rail the line was making too great a loss to continue. Bad management by BR did not help.

The closure saw the end to an era that had brought prosperity to Derbyshire. According to a report in the *Derby Advertiser* on 1 November 1963, Councillor J.H.Christmas accused BR of having discouraged rather than encouraged the use of the line. However, this gaslit piece of Derby's history was, in my opinion, doomed from the end of World War Two. It is too late now to dwell on why it closed, but many people who worked there can give their opinion, probably more accurately than British Rail. The purpose of this book is to share with you the stories of the people who worked and travelled from Friargate. Each has its own significance, from the childhood trips to the seaside, to the 4am shifts in the dead of winter, the shock of being told that a body had been found on the tracks outside Morley Tunnel, the joy of the train spotters who spent many happy hours in the refreshment room on the centre platform. I relate these stories as I was told them. People's memories do sometimes confuse facts, but that is all part of Friargate's history. What is important is people's fondness for the station.

I must thank all the people who telephoned or wrote to me, for together they bring the station back to life. Through them we can travel back to the days of steam, when train journeys were exciting, when nearly every boy dreamt of being an engine driver. The book begins with a brief history of how the station came about, then follow the memories of Friargate, and finally the photographs of the station, Slack Lane, Darley Grove and the factories and firms that were served by Friargate. The site of the station is now almost derelict, but if one looks closely, then it is not so difficult to imagine the station in its hey day. I hope you enjoy this book as much as I have enjoyed writing it.

Susan Bourne
Derby
March 1998

Friargate Gets Its Station

IN JULY 1872 The Great Northern Railway (Derbyshire and Staffordshire) Act came before Parliament. It began:

'An Act to enable the Great Northern Railway Company to construct Railways in Nottinghamshire and Derbyshire, and for other purposes with relation to the same Company.

'Whereas it is expedient that the Great Northern Railway (who are hereinafter referred to as "the Company") should be authorised to facilitate the communication between the Great Northern Railway on the one hand and Derbyshire and the North Staffordshire Railway near the southern terminus of that railway on the other hand, by the construction of the railways hereinafter described:

'And whereas it is also expedient that powers should be given to the Company on the one hand, and the London and North-Western and the North Staffordshire Railway Companies, or either of them, on the other hand, to enter into agreements as herein-after specified:

'And whereas plans and sections showing the lines and levels of the railways and other works authorised by this Act, and also books of reference containing the names of the owners and lessees, or reputed owners and lessees, and of the occupiers of the lands required or which may be taken for any of the purposes thereof, have been deposited with the clerks of the peace for the counties of Derby, Stafford, and Nottingham respectively, and are herein-after respectively referred to as the deposited plans, sections, and book of reference:

'And whereas the purposes of this Act cannot be effected without the authority of Parliament:

'May it therefore please Your Majesty that it may be enacted; and be it enacted by the Queen's most Excellent Majesty, by and with the advice and consent of the Lords Spiritual and Temporal, and Commons, in this present Parliament assembled, and by the authority of the same, as follows; (that is to say,)

1. This Act may be cited for all purposes as "The Great Northern Railway Short title.

(Derbyshire and Staffordshire) Act, 1872 …"

The Act received Royal Assent and by 1876 the Great Northern Railway Company was ready to expand into Derby. Although much opposition had been shown, Friargate was about to get its station. On 8 March that year the following announcement appeared in the *Derby Mercury* : 'The Great Northern Railway Company To Railway contractors. Derbyshire and North Staffordshire extension lines, construction of section No 4 through the town of Derby The directors of GNR company are prepared to receive tenders for the construction of the 4th section of the Derbyshire and North Staffordshire Railway authorised by the Act of 1872. This section comprises part of Railway No 7 described in the said Act about sixty chains in length commencing at the termination of contract No 3 in the Parish of St Alkmund's Derby and the termination on the south side of Friargate in the parish of St Werburgh's Derby in the county of Derbyshire. At the commencement of contract No 4, it includes also the construction of a passenger station at Friargate up to the level of platforms and a goods or coal yard at Duke Street, with sidings thereto. The working plans as prepared by Mr Richard Johnson may be seen on and after the 10th day of March instant, at the Engineer's office, King's Cross Station, London. Tenders sealed up and endorsed Tender for Derbyshire and North Staffordshire Extension Railways section No 4 should be addressed to the undersigned and deposited at the Secretary's office, King's Cross Station, London before twelve o'clock on Thursday the 6th day of April next, The directors do not bind themselves to accept the lowest tender.'

The Loss of the White Horse Tavern

THE building of Friargate Station inevitably meant that a significant area of Derby would be changed forever and the one building whose passing seems to have been mourned above all others was the White Horse Tavern. By the time the pub was demolished in 1876, the licensee Ann Taylor's family had occupied the premises for nearly a century. Her application to have her license transferred to premises nearby was refused by the magistrates. No reason was published. The following article appeared in the *Derby Mercury* of 3 February 1875 and is interesting, not only for its idyllic description of early Friargate, but for the fact that the White Horse comes to life as a quite notorious hostelry in the latter half of the 18th century.

The Poisoners of the 'Old White Horse Tavern'

FEW towns can boast of a finer or more striking entrance than that by which a traveller by the Queen's highway comes from the North into the ancient borough of Derby. Friar-gate, however, in 1732, was not much like the spacious well-built street which is one of the chief glories of modern Derby. It had not then lost the characteristics which are handed down to us by means of the queer plan of the town attached to Speed's map of 'Darbieshire' for changes were slow in coming here, until railways and Radicalism converted the little town, which Defoe described as 'a place of gentry rather than trade' (adding that what trade existed 'was chiefly in good ale') into a busy, commercial and manufacturing centre of industry. Quaint half-timbered houses, of Elizabethan aspect, looked out upon the green churchyard of St Werburgh's over the way, their upper stories projecting over the ill-paved causeway and affording shelter to the pedestrian in a sudden shower. Other lowly domiciles only boasted of one chamber above the ground-floor, and the latticed dormer windows peeped curiously out from amidst the thick thatch of the roof. There were but a few houses of red brick, most of which had lately been erected, and on the opposite side to the church the line of thatched roofs was only broken by the entrance gates and lodge of the Friary grounds. The relics of the old Dominican convent itself stood, far back from the street, in the midst of a pleasant park well-studded with stately trees, for Mr Crompton, who had recently become the possessor of this deserted nest of the Black Friars, had not yet utilised the materials in building the mansion which is familiar to every native of Derby under the name of 'The Friary'. A road skirted the churchyard and led by means of the Cuckstool bridge into St Mary's gate, an ominous path for women to travel since the bridge crossed a mill dam where the ducking-stool was erected; that terrible engine through whose means unruly wives were half-drowned into promises of obedience to their liege lords, by being soused hissing-hot into the clear waters of the Hodde brook On the west side of the street, the houses stood upon the crest of a gentle slope of gravel (long since cut away and used for road-making) a relic of which is to be seen in the elevated footpath, and in the steps by which the front doors of those dwellings are now gained. Brave beech trees lent a charming rural aspect to the scene, and, as the road widened out into the common known as Nuns Green, the houses became fewer and less important, and the roadside cross, so famous in Derby history, was seen to stand alone, by the side of the road, upon the waste. Old Hutton (let us remark, by way of digression) was not quite correct when he wrote that the inhabitants 'erected' this cross in 1665 for the especial, purpose of its serving as a medium betwixt buyer and seller during the perilous time of the Great Plague — it existed long before that period, and as the cattle and horse fairs had been held around it time out of mind, it was possibly a 'market-cross' to which our ancestors naturally enough resorted in that grim time of need. The Borough Gaol, before which, in later days, Brandreth and his wretched misguided companions paid the debt of ignorance with their lives, and which served Hutton to direct the attention of his reader to what he contemptuously styles 'a paltry public house', had not been planned. The common open to the brook, was intersected with streams and footpaths, and the most important structures which met the eye were the pinfold and a wretched prison in Willow-row. After passing the 'Headless Cross' the characteristics of the town began to lose themselves in those of the country; little cottages, built, perhaps, by adventurous 'squatters on the waste,' were dotted sparsely here and there and the road to Ashbourne lay for some distance between two rows of trees.

Amongst last of these dwellings which the traveller would pass as he left the town was the Old White Horse tavern, a hostelry which, almost unchanged in appearance, presents in 1875 a singular contrast with the brick houses which have sprung up around it. Here, the wayfarer could not fail to take a parting cup of the nut-brown ale (for which Derby was noted far and wide) always to be had in perfection at this homely roadside public-house, and the chances were that he would linger awhile to chat with the comely landlady, Mistress Ellen, or Eleanor Beare, 'A handsome woman,' says Rutten, 'of about thirty years of age, with an education superior to her rank, and mistress of that persuasive eloquence which insensibly wins over the hearer to the speaker's own side'. No one ever thought of conversing with Ebanezer Beare whilst the active busy wife was in the house eclipsing him with her presence and he seems to have been content with his position as a mere cipher under his own roof tree, which even went familiarly amongst the gossips by the name of 'Mrs Beare's'. Many a one, however, sought for the public-house near Headless Cross who were neither tempted by the excellence of the ale nor the charms of the landlady. It is true that their errand was mostly a secret between themselves and Mrs Beare, who, it was darkly whispered, dealt in other beverages, quite as potent and not nearly so wholesome as strong ale, and could furnish husbands who were, tired of their wives' clack with a less public and far more effectual method of stopping it for ever than even a ducking in the Cuck-stool mill-dam. Nor was her assistance withheld from her own sex under similar difficulties and if an indiscreet damsel wished to conceal her frailties from the prying eyes of her neighbours, or any married lady took a fancy to qualify herself for wearing a widow's cap, the landlady of the White Horse seldom disappointed those who reposed confidence in her skill.

Amongst the frequenters of the White Horse were a butcher, John Hewitt by name, and his wife who dwelt in Stepping-lane, hard by (Ford-street), and who were each heartily tired of the other's company. He was rather a favourite of the landlady, and of her waiting-maid, Rosamond Ollorenshaw, too; but poor Hannah Hewitt, who came stealthily and sought consolation in Mrs Beare's good ale from the cuffs and ill-usage of her husband, was only wearisome in her cups, always complaining of being half-starved at home whilst he enjoyed himself abroad — a very skeleton at the banquet. So good Mrs Beare, pitying the poor creature's forlorn state, consulted her handmaiden on the propriety of assisting her out of a world of woe, and the fair Rosamond having arrived, with butcher Hewitt, at the conclusion that when a vacancy occurred in Stepping-lane she should be called upon to fill it, entered 'with a light heart' upon the scheme. Where three parties were so well agreed it was not thought necessary to ask the opinion of the fourth, and when, one Saturday, unhappy Hannah Hewitt came into the White Horse with the usual complaint of being clammed at home, what more natural than for the kind-hearted landlady who was getting ready for Shrovetide, to invite her guest to eat a pancake in advance of that festive season? It was her last meal, for, in three hours after Mrs Beare's hospitality to his wife, John Hewitt was free to marry Rosamond Ollorenshaw without fear of a prosecution for bigamy.

The skill of the Derby Borgia seems to have failed her at last, or her eagerness in this instance deprived her of caution; for a death so sudden, and so environed with the horrors of rapid, irritant poisoning, could not fail to arouse suspicion; the neighbours cried Foul play! the Coroner was summoned and a post-mortem examination revealed arsenic enough to have served Mrs Beare for half-a-dozen of her peculiar patients instead of one only. Then, a public outcry arose, and almost with the avowed object of sparing Mr Justice Lynch a task (for which he was quite prepared), all parties were taken on Sunday night and lodged in the prison in the Corn-market, which standing, then, on a site now occupied by part of the Royal Hotel buildings, gave its name to the Jail Bridge spanning the brook at this point.

The assizes took place soon afterwards and the historian observes that at the trial of the poisoners, Hewitt, finding that his doom was sealed, tried to save Rosamond, who seems to have been questioned in a manner not altogether in accordance with modern law; but Hutton shall here speak for himself: 'It is probable Hewitt had an affection for Rosamond, for the Judge having asked her whether Mrs Beare was privy to the poisoning or ordered her to administer it, John trod upon her toe in order that she might tell the truth and save herself, but she unfortunately mistook the hint for its reverse and answered No, by which she saved the life of her mistress and lost her own.' Mrs Beare was acquitted, and her two less guilty associates were condemned to be executed. What follows presents a curious picture of Derby manners and customs nearly a century and a half ago. Samuel Drewry had (just about this period of our story), started a newspaper called *The Derby Mercury* of which he issued 'the first Paper *gratis* by way of Specimen' on the 23rd of March, 1732. The first regular number which follows is dated 'No. 1, Thursday, March 30, 1732,' and furnishes the following particulars, which we re-print *verbatim et literim*

> Derby, March 29. This day John Hewitt and Rosamond Ollorenshaw were executed here in pursuance of the Sentence passed upon 'em at the last Assizes for poisoning Hannah Hewitt, the wife of John Hewitt. They confess'd their being guilty soon after Condemnation and have since appeared very penitent. The Day before the Execution they each of 'em signed an open Confession of their Crimes and gave it to the Printer of this Paper and to no other to be publish'd as a Warning to Others (it was accordingly printed and is now very much bought up). The Rev. Mr Locket preached to the prisoners on the 27th inst from *Matt.* 24, 44 — *Be ye also ready* — And on the 28th the Rev. Mr Cantrell preach'd to them from *Acts* 3 and 19 — *Repent and be converted,* &c. These Divines also attended them to the Place of Execution.

To hear these sermons the condemned prisoners were taken from the gaol to St Peter's Church, and Hutton remarks that Rosamond, being heavily fettered and half-dead with the apprehension of her approaching fate, could scarcely rise from her knees, whereupon Hewitt 'took her round the waist in the face of a crowded church and tenderly raised her'. They walked to the place of execution (probably on the road to Normanton, although at the latter end of the 17th century the gallows stood upon Nun's Green), and Hutton is careful to record that Hewitt wore a suit of dark grey with black cuffs and trimmings, and that his unfortunate partner in crime hung upon his arm dressed in a drab gown and a hat which nearly covered her face. *The Derby Mercury* mentions the fact that Hewitt took a book with him entitled 'An Account of the Life and Death of Thomas Savage' 'and read in it most part of the way, which is not quite consistent with one's ideas of a walking procession; but both authorities agree in stating, as a singular circumstance, that each, upon arriving at the gallows stripped off their upper clothing, and presented themselves to the awe-struck gaze of 'vast numbers of people who pitied and prayed for them;' attired in their grave-clothes 'There,' says the old journalist, 'both of 'em warned the Spectators, especially the younger People, to beware of bad Company and all wicked Temptations. J. Hewitt said if he had a thousand Worlds he would give them all so he might lead his life over again. It is hardly to be conceived with what Earnestness he continued praying for Mercy till the Cart was drawn away.'

What became, of the Landlady of the White Horse? Thereby hangs another tale which would be tedious to repeat at length here. She was seized in the night of the same day which witnessed the death of her wretched dupes and an indictment was preferred against her at the next assizes, held at Derby on Tuesday, August 13th before Mr Justice Price, for 'endeavouring to persuade John Wilson to poison his wife, and for giving him poison for that end,' and other charges scarcely less atrocious. These crimes being only known to the law of that day as 'misdemeanours' this 'wholesale dealer in human destruction' as Hutton calls her, was condemned to stand twice in the pillory the two first market days and suffer close imprisonment for three years. Hutton gives a graphic account of the terrible handling she received whilst pilloried on August 18th, at the hands of the enraged multitude; and from him we learn that at the close of her imprisonment, she, 'having recovered her health, her spirits, and her beauty,' was escorted home by the fickle populace in triumphal procession, preceded by a band of music. Our readers will agree with us in thinking that the annals of crime present few more striking examples than the career of the poisoners of the 'Old White Horse' tavern in Friar-gate, a house which will soon be swept away before the advance of the Great Northern Railway through Derby.

Memories of Friargate Station

ON a freezing, snowy day in February 1996, together with my son, I stumbled along an overgrown path to see what was left of Friargate Station. We walked along the snow-covered platform where once so many people had gathered, where excited children had once stood impatiently, buckets and spades at the ready, waiting for the train, which would transport them to the seaside. Not for them the soulless, impersonal people carriers of today, but huge glorious black monsters belching steam, and that unmistakable smell of burning coal that gave rise to emotions of both terror and excitement in equal proportions. We could almost hear those happy voices long past, and as steam rose from the workshops below the former station, the distant sound of a braking motor car for a moment sounded like a train whistle. We looked along the platform half expecting the big black train to pull into the station. Our imagination was working overtime and we both laughed at our foolishness, but I swear for a moment I did see that train, maybe the last train to leave the station all those years ago.

Today, most people think that all that remains of the station is the handsome wrought-iron bridge which spans Friargate, now restored but its future still uncertain. If the site is finally redeveloped it may have to go, but hopefully it will be retained as a feature, as I hope will be the now-listed Goods Depot. If one looks carefully there is still a lot left, as the photographs in this book show. The platforms, although overgrown, are still recognisable as such, although the rails have long gone. Even the exit to the centre platform from the subway is still there. The huge majestic Goods Depot, like an abandoned ocean liner, stands alone, derelict. The old engine house has been much abused over the years but at least it is still in use, as a workshop to make pinewood furniture. Back to street level, the arches are now workshops and garages. The subway garage still has the entrance to the subway to the island platform, its steps this side gone but the tiles still in place. The arches lead right through to the other side to where Mike Cordon has his car sales business. The main entrance to the station can still be seen and, as can be seen from photographs, is very little changed. The water lift is in part still there, gaily painted. And if one walks back along where the tracks would have been, there is much more still, which I will describe later.

It is over thirty years since Friargate Station finally closed, but people's memories are long and so many people have stories to tell. It was not just a working station but a place where important journeys began, where everyday people went to and from work. During two world wars, troops embarked for their various postings, often leaving behind tearful families. Some of those servicemen never returned.

Mrs F. Siddons recalls travelling from Friargate Station in 1943 with her two young children, then aged three and four. Her husband was stationed in Norfolk and to see him she had to get a train to Grantham, then one to Peterborough before finally arriving in Sheringham at 8 o'clock at night. Later he was stationed at Weybourne. The family she stayed with had no electricity supply in their house and they had to draw all their water from the bottom of a big hill. Her husband was lucky and he did return. Sadly he has now passed away but Mrs Siddons wrote that she has many happy memories of Friargate, as, I would imagine, do her children.

During World War Two, Friargate Station must have been exceptionally busy, for the huge Goods Depot was used to store supplies for the American Army. **Mr Les Sayers** told me how he started work on the station during the war, when he was just 14. He was an apprentice in the Derby East Signal Box, under the supervision of a Mr Bader, and he can remember travelling to Nottingham every day, for what seemed like an eternity, on the 9.12am from Friargate, arriving in Nottingham Victoria around 10 o'clock. He learnt Morse code, which he thought he would never master but which he can still do today, if a little more slowly than when he was a boy just starting out on his working life. He would arrive back at Friargate around 5pm, on a train filled with office and mill girls (a young man's dream!). He also recalls using the water lift which was operated from the subway, the water coming from St Mary's Wharf. Horses and carts were still in use, lodged in the stables under the arches or across the road at the Tram Depot. He recalls being keen on a girl who worked in the offices at the Goods Depot, where access to the offices was via a spiral staircase. And during the war there were women linesmen as most of the men were away in the services. He remembers going across to a shop on Friargate to obtain meat for the station cats. The meat was not considered fit for human consumption and was dyed green so that people wouldn't eat it. Sometime the cats wouldn't be quick enough and there would be the awful sight of one cut in half by a passing train.

Mike Cordon, who has been trading at the arches since the early 1960s, recalls how on a Saturday, children would gather wide-eyed around the sleek sports cars. In those days, he told me, he could leave the cars open and not worry about vandalism. The only damage was when a metal bucket would occasionally chip some paintwork.

The Goods Depot was a hive of industry and **Mr Maurice Oakley** recalls: "During the early 1950s I worked as a railway clerk at the large goods warehouse. I was responsible for the control of the large stock of grain, cattle foods and sugar, which were held and distributed from there. I dealt with many reps and customers collecting stocks from Appleton's, BOCM, Spillers and others including the British Sugar Corporation. Stocks came in by rail and were off-loaded by the railway staff employed there at the time. This was a very interesting job dealing with so many different people. The warehouse was at that time lit by gas lights in the office, but even so we managed okay. Stocktaking was, of course a daylight job!

"Pre-war I remember as a young man the LNER used to run a Sunday service to Skegness. I think it cost two shillings and sixpence. It departed after lunch, gave about four hours in Skegness and arrived back at Friargate around midnight …The trains used to run through Breadsall and Ilkeston and we used to look for the old Boston Stump — then we knew we were well on the way to Skeggy. The Sunday trip was well patronised."

The station has fond memories for **Mrs Rosemary York**: "When I was a child in the 1920s and 30s, my parents used to take my brother and myself on day excursions and also on our annual holiday to the East Coast. I remember we had to climb a long flight of steps from Friargate to reach the platform. The carriages were non-corridor so there were no toilet facilities on this journey!"

More childhood memories come from **Mrs W.O'Donnell**: "As a child I lived near the station, and its familiar noises — trains rumbling over the bridge, shunting, clanging and whistles blowing, and the night noises from the trains — was a part of our lives. I knew a Mr Fred Dainty, a porter at the station. He lived in Merchant Street and to see him coming down Markeaton Street in his black uniform with silver buttons, carrying his lunch box, was an everyday sight. He looked to me as if he enjoyed his job and was very proud of the station. He was a good gardener, I remember, and probably used his skills on the platform garden. The excitement of going to that little station, mostly for trips to Skegness, is something I'll never forget. Nowhere else compares to it — the little booking hall to the right and the walk in semi-darkness under the actual station, and the smell of fish in the warehouse, probably coming in from Grimsby. Then up the stone steps and on to the platform to wait for the train. It was another world, so thrilling and at the same time homely and tranquil."

Mr Percy Sims, who at over 90 still has good recall of his time at the station, told me. During the severe winter of 1947 he helped to dig the trains out of snowdrifts sometimes over l4ft in height, but the trains still managed to get through! He recalls that he moved to Friargate from Birmingham when his father died. He brought his father's cottage which was ten miles from the station, in a place called Two Fields. He drove to work for ten years. He worked shifts, one from 4am to 4pm and another which started at 1pm until approximately 10.l5pm. He drove the last double-headed express trains. He had previously worked at Midland Road, but didn't like it there. He recalls bagging trains up with snow-ploughs in winter, and how reliable the old steam trains were. World War Two was still raging when he first transferred from Birmingham, and for a while he had to lodge in Derby. This was in the March and his wife did not join him until August. They have now been married for 66 years. He also remembers a friend who had a shed on the site where he made motorbikes which he exported to India. Mr Sims' eyesight is very poor now and this he blames in part on the sparks that used to fly into his face when train pulled into the station, and the firemen shovelled on the coal, whereupon the coal dust would ignite and burn the faces of those close by.

Mr Sims retired at 61, just before the station closed.

Mr Cresswell, a porter and shunter, worked at Friargate Station in 1937. He often endured a cold, wet journey in winter as he travelled the nine miles to work from Wainsgrove near Ripley on a motorbike. Some mornings he had to leave home at 4am. He worked one 12-hour shift, starting at 5am, and another shift which started at 1.15pm and lasted until 10.15pm, when the last train arrived from Burton upon Trent. Before he finished he had to make sure the trains were in the engine shed. He recalls that one morning, on an early shift, he was told that a body had been found outside Morley Tunnel. The platelayers moved the body, much to his relief as he certainly didn't want to see it. He also recalls that when he worked on the Racecourse, two women were killed outside the Signal Box. Apparently the weather was poor and although a warning shout was heard, they were hit by an express. It was during a November race meeting, he thinks, around 1937. He also remembers the 11.15am from Hull, filled with fresh fish for Derby Fish Market, and that it had to be swept out before it could be used as the 5.37pm passenger train. He started work at 13 as a shunter at his local pit. At Friargate he was a porter as there were no vacancies for shunters, although he did work overtime as a shunter at weekends. Mr Cresswell is now over 90.

Mr Seaman worked at the Loco Works at Slack Lane from 1946 to 1964. At Slack Lane there was a skin yard where animal skins were cured. There was a large engine shed that held six to eight engines. His wife also worked on the Friargate line as a cleaner on the station. The livery of GNR was mainly black with yellow lettering. Some coaches were dark green. There were corridor and non-corridor coaches at the station. He worked on the midweek trips to the coast and also at weekends and he recalls that this was always a busy time. The trips were always full with up to nine coaches on during the summer. During World War Two the Goods Depot was used by the American Army to store ammunition. After the war it was used for food stuffs, including pet foods. The small outbuilding attached to the back of the warehouse was apparently a pump-house and the round mound of bricks, to the right of the warehouse (see photographs), was the site of a crane. During his time on the line he was a fireman and a driver. He gave me his reasons why he thought Friargate had finally closed — a firemen's strike that lasted 3 weeks. The union wanted a rise for both firemen and drivers (there were 16 drivers and 15 firemen). Apparently the union only got a rise for the drivers and nine fiiremen handed in their notice on the same day. BR had to bring extra firemen from Nottingham, who received double pay which put up cost of operating the line. These men would travel to Derby on the cushions return to Nottingham the same way. When his son was old enough, his wife would wait by the bridge on Old Uttoxeter Road and he would pick up his son and take him for a ride up the line — every young boy's dream.

One amusing story was recalled by **John Roe**, whose father was the last station master at Friargate. During World War Two, troops as well as civilians used the line and they would all pile on the trains together. Friargate was gas-lit and when the train pulled into the station, the ticket collector had a lamp. Invariably someone would blow out his lamp, leaving him in semi-darkness as tickets were thrust into his hand. On checking them later, he would find bus tickets, platform tickets and out-of-date used train tickets. The soldiers, of course, all had travel passes. The rest? Well, there was a war on!

During the 1950s, **Alan Rimmer,** many of whose photographs appear in the book, worked as a member of BR Research. He was also an avid trainspotter from the mid-1940s and took many photographs around the Friargate Station and the Locomotive Depot. He has an enduring memory of the very pleasant Refreshment Room at the top of the steps on the centre platform. He and a friend spent many pleasant evenings between watching the trains. He also got to know the signalman in the Friargate West box, although alas, after all this time he can't recall his name.

The Residence

by Sybil Ride

TO RETURN to the earlier part of Friargate's history, I had a lovely letter from Lynda Ride, whose 75-year-old mother-in-law had asked her to type up some childhood memories. She, too, has very clear memories of the station and its surrounding area. She moved to Friargate in 1928 when the station was at its best and busiest. Her family moved into the Goods Depot, where there was living accommodation on the third floor of the building, and offices for station staff below. Her memories bring the station to life as no photograph can:

"The passenger train chugged its way into the small but cleanly swept station at Friargate, Derby. It snorted to a halt at the end of the platform, hissing and belching steam. We had travelled from Nottingham, myself, Mother and my two sisters, Hilda who was the eldest, and Audrey. Then Dad was there, lifting us down from the train to the platform one by one, and finally helping Mother down the steps, which always seemed such a long way down from the train to the platform.

"As we stood there, our little family group, Dad pointed out a large building that we could see in the distance, which from that day we would be calling The Residence. First Dad took us into the town and left us at the Museum and Library, whilst he went to fetch his case from the lodgings he had stayed in for a few weeks, until he had at last found somewhere for us to live. I was barely seven years old and to me the Museum had a funny musty smell. When you talked it seemed to echo round the large rooms, so we wrinkled our noses and whispered.

"I was glad Dad wasn't too long coming for us, and happy to be on the pavement again. It was a short walk from the Museum, along Curzon Street to Stafford Street, where we came to two large cream-painted gates and a smaller wicket gate. On the right, as we all trooped through the small gate, were huge piles of wood, seasoning Dad said. It was a builder's yard and across to the left was a low-slung building, which was a weighing office. Dad explained that the cart loads of goods had to be weighed before they were taken to be delivered. You see, the large building was a railway goods depot. There was a grey roadway sloping up from the large gates, winding its way round, and in between a rather nice area of grass, finally losing itself to a cobbled part, which was fronted by the huge 'Goods Depot' words , high up on a cream supporting girder.

"On the left of the cobbled area was a small well-built structure which was to be our coal house. On the right-hand side was a small pavement, a gas lamp on the wall and two glass-panelled doors, through which we stepped on to a paved slabbed area. Doors led off, and stairs, going both down and up, up, up, 52 steps up to our front door. This was also glass-panelled, the top half that is, and the word 'Private' was nicely painted in gold lettering, which I rather liked. Dad unlocked the door and opened it for Mother, and we all went in. There was a spacious hall which led to a smaller passage, with three doors leading off. The one on the right was to be the girls' room, the one at the end was to be Mother and Dad's room, while the one on the right would make a very nice best room.

"This room was a funny shape, something like a sock shape, and it had four windows. The living room was also a strange shape, with a coal-fired range, a built-in cupboard from floor to ceiling, and also a table which let down to hang against the wall, so that it was out of the way. There was also a huge floor-to-ceiling built-in Welsh dresser.

"The scullery led off this room and in this was a copper for boiling up on wash day. Next to this was a brown glazed sink with one cold water tap. A small pantry was off the left-hand wall of the scullery, while shelves ran along the longest wall span. The cost of this flat was six shillings a week. The gas fittings were to be regularly serviced and two rooms were to be decorated every two years, with paintwork and paper of Mother's own choosing, free of charge.

"I should mention the toilet, which was off the hall to the left. It was built-in wall-to-wall. It had a large mahogany lid and the pan itself was encased in red mahogany. In the ceiling was a fan-light which was operated by a cord. The removal van arrived and we were in. Our bedroom was oblong in shape, with one window in the far end wall. It had a gaslight which was switched on and off by small chains which had to be pulled down. On the opposite wall was a fireplace and a built-in wardrobe. My sisters had a double brass bedstead and I had a smaller one. There was also room for the washstand, with its jug and bowl, the dressing table and matching wardrobe and cane-seat bedroom chair.

"The wallpaper Mother chose for our room was small pretty lanterns hanging on leaves, on a white background. The paint was also white. We had two pictures on the wall. The one above my sister's bed was called *Sunset on the Common* and above mine was *The Blind Fiddler*.

"Our parents' room was more or less square. They had a wooden head and tailboard bed, a small table, chair and built-in wardrobe and also two pictures, something to do with a ploughman and his horses.

"The best room was well scrubbed out and eventually linoleum was laid. A four-by-three carpet was chosen and put down and then a three-piece suite and sideboard. The wallpaper Mother had chosen for this room was a pretty leaf pattern of blues and silver on a white background. There was a gaslight and a fireplace. This room had four windows and Mother made all the curtains for each room. It took a roll of material, nicely patterned, flowers on a white background.

"The living room walls were painted brown halfway up, then papered, with a border running round the top and bottom edges. This paper was pink blossom on a fawn background, with dark branches picking up the brown of the paintwork.

"The built-in Welsh dresser was washed down and polished. Soon the best dinner service was displayed on it and also the everyday one, and other crockery in use every day. The flooring was wood-block patterned linoleum with the four-by-three cord carpet. On this stood the draw-leaf dinning table, its polished surface protected by a special cover, and also table mats when we had hot meals.

"Soon, a table-top wooden washing machine was bought and installed in the scullery. You had to put the clothes in a wooden drum and then hot water, boiled in the copper, was ladled and bucketed into the washing machine.

"Soap powder was put in, two lids placed on top and the drum was revolved by pushing a wooden handle back and forth for some time until the clothes were clean. There was a tap to empty the water into buckets and, this done, clean water was put in and the drum revolved again. In this way the clothes were rinsed. A mangle was attached to one end of the machine which squeezed the water out of the clothes most efficiently. The fire hole underneath the copper then had to be raked out when the ashes had cooled down. The ashes were put on the living room fire — all the rubbish was burned on this fire. The coal to feed it had to be carried up the 52 steps from the coal house down below. The steps were broken up by small landings.

There was a longer landing leading to our front door, and one which led to the roof to the left. Dad used to fill an old tin trunk twice a week with coal so Mother didn't have to carry any. We girls would carry the odd bucket up, when Mother needed it and Dad wasn't there. The washing was dried on lines on the roof of the residence. These were fastened to three chimneys and sometimes it was very windy. Up there you were above the roof tops of Derby and you could see all the church towers and spires.

"The Goods Depot was a very busy place, with wagons being shunted in and out and horse-drawn drays coming and going all day long. Each side of the building had sidings into which, day and night, wagons were being shunted. It was a very comforting sound if you awoke during the night. As the wagons caught each other up, a musical sound went from engine to buffers — ting-tang, ting-tang it went. There was the roadway which curved around the buffers to the left, and this had little wooden huts strewn along, mostly for coal merchants. There was always a heap of scrap metals waiting to be loaded too. Sometimes there were wagons loaded with bones. You could see rib-cages and skulls of cattle. I didn't like to see them. Sometimes they were covered with tarpaulins, but the bones still poked out. Porters, the corn and seed merchants, had a stoutly-built wooden shed at the front of the buffers to the right of the Depot. Following the road round there was the station, so we were the real railway children, with a station and real trains in what you might call our back-yard.

"The stables for the horses were underneath the station and one day Mr Swain, who was in charge of the stables, took my sisters and I to see them. I remember there was a horse in a stall at the far end who wasn't well. He was covered with sacks and looked very dejected. I felt sorry for him and so wanted him to feel better quite soon. Next to the stables under the station was a candle-making factory and one day we were taken to see the candles being made. It was a dimly-lit place and I remember the candles taking shape in wax-filled troughs which moved gently. The workers looked pale in the eerie light and it looked as if it was a dirty job. There was a green area in front of the factory with shrubs and small trees in it.

"When the circus came to Derby they were unloaded in one of the sidings and small crowds would come to watch this. The animals were paraded through the streets to where they were being stabled for the period of the show. This was always an exciting event. One Sunday there was an American lion-tamer and he had to supervise the unloading of his lions. There was only my sisters and myself around, playing on the grass, and he came to us and asked if there was anywhere he and his wife could get a cup of tea. I was thrilled to say my Mother would make one for them, gladly. So I dashed upstairs, leaving my sisters to show them the way, and in a breathless fashion I told Mother about the lion-tamer. I asked, could she make them a cup of tea and could I please take it in to them? So Mother busied herself with the tea making and we girls ushered our guests into the best room. Mother went in to meet them and I was allowed to take the tray in for them, with orders to come away and leave them to have their tea in peace. Mother chatted to them for a few minutes and as he left the lion-tamer slipped a shilling into my hand, which I shared with my sisters. Mother always made me do that. Needless to say we all went to see his show, which was at the Hippodrome Variety Theatre. The lion-tamer had a large cage on stage and he wore a gold-braided uniform. We all felt very proud to have actually met him.

"You may wonder how we came to be living at the The Residence. Well, Dad was a driver for the LNE Railway. When he was off duty, he had to go to an office in the engine shed to collect his wages and sometimes he would take me with him. One day we came back on the footplate of an engine and I was allowed to pull the whistle. I wasn't keen to ride on the footplate again, it was far too hot for me, I could hardly breathe.

"Dad used to bring a large block of salt home during the winter months and we girls used to grate it fine and put it into a large tin, and jars. It would take us a few evenings to do this.

"When we came home from school we had to change from our gym-slips into play clothes. On a Monday, which was always Mother's washing day, I would come home from school, change, and then I would rake the cold ashes out from under the copper, a job I quite enjoyed doing really. My sisters would help to wash the scullery shelves and put clean newspapers on them for the cooking pans. We would all sing together and amid much laughter the work was done.

"We took it in turns to scrub Dad's overalls in the brown sink. When they were dried and ironed we would sew on any buttons that had come off. Dad used to say that those we sewed on never came off, but we used to think it was to get us to sew them on in the first place. He always carried a couple of safety pins on him, which he called his spare parts.

"We kept our bedroom clean and tidy, washing finger marks off the white paintwork and dusting. Polishing the linoleum was great fun. We used to put my sister Audrey on a large clean polishing up cloth and swing her to and fro under the beds and much giggling and laughing ensued. Also the linoleum shone like polished glass. Hilda, my elder sister, and I also used to tie dusters over our feet and skate all round the rest of the linoleum, amid squeals of delight.

"Mother made almost everything we ate or drank. She made wine for any visitors we had. One night, after trying some parsnip wine she had made, she went to bed. During the night there occurred an earth tremor, which shook Mother's bed. She thought it was the wine she had tasted and it was a family joke for a very long time. Mother made all kinds of sweets. Toffee which had to be pulled over a hook whilst it was still hot and pliable, then rolled and cut into bite-sizes pieces. She also made tray toffee, raisin candy, fudge with nuts, and for winter cough candy. Lovely lemon and barley water and nettle beer were also home made.

"Dad used to clean the widows outside by sitting on the window ledge. I was terrified that he might fall so I used to hang on to his legs to make sure he wouldn't, as if my puny weight would have held him! One day he was cleaning the inside of the scullery window, which was above the copper on which he stood, when he stepped back too far, fell off and really hurt himself.

"There was another time we were all worried for him. Mother told us Dad had been walking down the line from the engine shed (Friargate Shed) on his way home with another driver, and with talking hadn't noticed an engine bearing down on them. Dad, just in time, pulled the other man down to the ground with him as the engine went over them. Dad and his friend were unhurt but white with shock.

"One evening it was very windy and Mother was burning the usual rubbish on the fire when suddenly the chimney caught fire. Mother put a lot of the burning rubbish and hot coals into a large bucket and carefully took it outside on to the stone landing. We girls were left to throw salt onto the rest of the fire and fireback but burning soot kept falling. Mother dashed downstairs and across the railway yard to see if she could get help. Fortunately Dad was on his engine in the shunting area and he dashed back with Mother.

"Grabbing a couple of buckets and a large saucepan they dashed up to the roof and Mother filled the buckets from the tank up there. This was the water tank which supplied the engines from the station with their water. Dad managed to put the fire out and we girls were mopping up the rivulets of sooty water. The salt had quietened the remaining coals in the grate.

"We did not light a fire again until the chimney was swept. The chimneys were far too high and wide for ordinary chimney sweep's rods and brushes. What Mother and Dad did was to make a huge bundle of straw with two clothes lines tied to it. Dad went up on the roof again and dropped the end of one line down to Mother. When she had hold of the line and had fixed sacking and sheets round the fire-range, they pulled the bundle of straw up and down the chimney. It did a very good job because that was the way the chimney was swept ever after.

"Mother was always very strict with us girls, I suppose she had to be, living were we did, so that she would know we wouldn't go near the wagons and trains. But we accepted everything around us as quite normal. The busyness of the place was exciting. There were about nine maintenance men who came now and then to do work on the roof, and painting jobs. Some of their wives would visit Mother, and we would play with their children.

"Mother always took us for a day to Skegness. She also took two schoolfriends of ours and the charlady's daughter. The charlady was a widow who cleaned the offices which were below us at The Residence. We all used to have a lovely time paddling and playing on the sands."

"There was about nine cats in the big warehouse and one we girls called Billy, but who Mother called Minnie. She was a lovely looking tabby cat. You couldn't pick her up, but if you knelt down she would sometimes condescend to walk on to our knees. She had kittens in my sister Audrey's doll's pram, which was kept on the landing. Of course it had to be destroyed when the cat had finished with it. Another time she had her kittens down in the cellars. She brought them up the 52 steps to show them to us and how she managed it we just couldn't believe.

"We came home from school one day to find the stair banisters decorated and some activity in one of the offices. Dashing up the rest of the stairs we asked Mother if she knew what was going on. When she told us the Railway Queen was being crowned, oh the excitement! Could we go and see? Only if we were very quiet and didn't get in anyone's way, we were told. My sister Hilda was too shy to come with me, so I went down by myself into the office which was full of men all smartly dressed in their best suits. No one said anything to me so I moved closer to watch. I thought the young woman who had been chosen looked lovely in a long dress, scarlet cloak and train. She held a bouquet of flowers and was crowned. Speeches followed and I dashed back to Mother and Hilda to tell them all about it.

"Another time, on arriving home from school Mother told us about the *R101* airship flying past darkening the living room. She thought there was going to be a storm, but on looking out of the window she saw it was the airship. My age was about nine or ten. I am now 75."

I thank Mrs Ride for her invaluable insight to what it was like to live in the Goods Depot. Looking at the building today it is hard to imagine people living there, but with this lovely account we can share a little of what it must have been like. I took some photographs of the offices and living accommodation in early 1997. Parts of it now are too unsafe to enter and although I would love to explore it properly, sadly the building has been left to rot. Even though some attempts have been made to block the entrances up, the main wooden doors at the side have been left open, a perfect invitation to the mindless vandals that now roam the building. All that will be left are the memories of the people that lived and worked there, or like me, want to preserve something of Derby's history before it is too late.

Departure from Friargate

By Alan Rimmer

"THE early morning of Saturday, 23 December 1944 was dank, cold and foggy. Really foggy with visibility down to about ten yards in places. I walked down Duffield Road, Lodge Lane, and Ford Street to reach Friargate just before seven in the morning. There were no street lights as it was still wartime and the swirling vapours accentuated the darkness. I turned along Friargate, under the railway bridge and turned left up the station approach. There was a glimmer of light from the gaslight above the booking office window, through which a more brightly-lit interior could be seen.

"I should perhaps explain that I had started work some 15 months earlier as an apprentice in the LMS Locomotive Works at Derby. In that time, I had developed an interest in locomotives, and became a number snatcher! Not just crossing out or ticking numbers in an ABC, (in fact Ian Allan was only just getting into his stride with these little books). His LMS lists came out in December 1944, following on from the Southern lists, which had come out two years earlier. Anyway, at that time I noted every number in a notebook, and subsequently transferred everything into a loose-leaf file, noting also the date and where the engine was seen. The purpose of today's journey was to go with a fellow apprentice to Doncaster and York, where we hoped to get into the engine sheds.

"But back to Friargate. As a railway employee, I had filled in a privilege ticket form, which had been duly authorised, and which I now passed to the booking clerk. He pulled a ticket from the rack. I heard the 'Ker-lonck, Ker-lonck' as he dated it. I passed over my money, took the precious piece of paste-board and turned, through the tunnel under the platform and up the staircase on the right. At that time in the morning the Refreshment Room was still closed. At the platform was a train of five coaches with D2 4-4-0 at its head. It was wreathed in steam, adding to the fog, and here and there along the train, steam from the heating pipes rose up the side of the train. Occasionally, there was a glow of light from the engine footplate as the fireman opened the door to put in more coal. Canvas screens between cab roof and tender helped to minimise light straying upwards.

"Ghostly figures moved around the platform, lit only by dim, screened, gas lamps, which cast little pools of light and left stretches of darkness between them. Goods were being loaded into the guards van, and someone was waiting with his bicycle to be put aboard. I climbed into an empty compartment, lit by a single small bulb with about the power of two candles. The window blinds were all pulled down, and I let the one up on the door, and lowered the window. As I looked out, the luggage compartment doors slammed shut. A porter told me I must pull the blind down as soon as we set off, which I said I would do. He turned towards the rear of the train, and there was a gleam of green from the guard's oil lamp and a piercing blast on his whistle. The porter turned towards the engine, raised his arm and shouted, "Right Away". There was a squeal from the engine whistle (a squeal is the only description one can apply to the Great Northern whistle note). A jolt as the couplings took the stain and we moved off into the swirling mist over the bridge. The exhaust beats increased in speed as the train rumbled over the arches of the viaduct, then plunged beneath the group of bridges which carried Duffield Road (King Street), Edward Street, Arthur Street, North Street and North Parade over the line. Across the arched bridge over the River Derwent, and along the embankment behind the houses on Chester Green. Then we were on the viaduct over the LMS line, and the Little Eaton branch of the Derby Canal, reaching the other side of the valley and climbing towards Breadsall. Dawn was just starting to lighten the day as we made our way, calling at Breadsall, West Hallam, Ilkeston, Awsworth, Kimberley, Basford and Bulwell and New Basford. Our progress was slow, obviously because of the fog, and we finally reached Nottingham Victoria about 40 minutes late. I had missed my connection, and there was no sign of my companion for the day. The day was retrieved, as I went on to Grantham and Doncaster, and ended up meeting Terry at York. But the days events from Nottingham onwards are another story.

"Again only the people who travelled from Friargate will know this journey, and I hope it brings back pleasant memories for you. Many people preferred to travel from Friargate, even though it took longer than from Midland Road, as it was a more interesting journey."

Dark Nights, Summer Saturdays and Schooldays

by Ken Cook

"Many an autumn and winter night was spent in the old wooden waiting room on the island platform at the top of the entrance hall stairs. It was more or less a Friargate GN enthusiasts' club, or at least somewhere to shelter on cold evenings! The die-hard rail enthusiasts (who normally congregated at the Five-Arches on the Midland line) included myself, Gary Warrington, Pete Riley, Joe Cartledge, Pete Rook, Peter 'Doors' Kimpton, Mick Page and others.

"The waiting room fire was well fed with coal and every now and then the station porter would come in to check on things. The rumble of an old freight train would break the silence and the operating highlights of the evening would be the local train from Grantham (hauled by L1 class or Ivatt 2-6-O [Pig] which would deposit a handful of passengers before returning to Nottingham, usually with just one or two passengers — they were called passengers in those days, not customers — boarding. And a typical evening of spotting is: From 6-15pm-9.00pm. Locos recorded 61229, 43090, 67800, 90349.

"In the '50s and '60s a lot of Derby people spent their holidays on the Lincolnshire coast, so trains from Friargate were the obvious choice for transport. On a Saturday morning there were a variety of trains to Mablethorpe, Skegness. For the more adventurous there were Friday night (10.30, 11.30) services to Bournemouth and Ramsgate (via the Great Central). Saturday morning was a busy scene with Black Arrow taxis depositing holidaymakers on the station forecourt. Suitcases, buckets and spades, children — it was all part of the scene. After 11.00am the station again was tranquil, until about 4.00pm when the return journeys would bring back hundreds of returning holidaymakers.

"Being a pupil at the old Derby School had its advantages if you had any sort of interest in railways. From the top floor, if you opted for a window desk, one could keep one eye on the blackboard and the other a birds' eye view of Friargate Station and the line up to King Street. If you happened to be in the physics lab or the chapel, when a train passed under the bridge, the whole place used to vibrate!

"Sporting activities at the City Road (Parker's Piece) Sports Field was afforded a splendid view of the line with the embankment bordering the playing field. One event sticks in my memory regarding the Handyside River Bridge which was at the end of the sports field. Derby School had its own Army Cadet Corps and one practice operation was to pretend to blow up the bridge using very low-powered explosives. One of the cadets roped himself to the bridge, set the detonating timer and was then supposed to lower himself down into a boat, then …wait for the bang. However, the rope got stuck, so there was immediate panic and some swearing etc before he eventually decided to jump into the river. As the explosion sounded, a coal train came over the bridge with the driver hanging out of the cab window, wondering what was going on. At the same time the cadet hit the river below!"

More Memories

LOOKING at the Friargate site now it is hard to imagine what life was like on the station, which for almost 80 years it had its own traditions and celebrations. Generations of Derby people grew up around the station and it was a focal point for many people. **Miss E. Holmes**, who is now 93 years old, recalls: "My Grandad and Grandma came from Dover to work on the bridge (Friargate). He was an engineer, quite famous in his day, and his name was Samuel. When he retired he was given a purse of gold and a gold-mounted umbrella for Grandma. I walk under the bridge often and it seems part of me. They had a railway house in Granville Street and later they moved to 45 Uttoxeter Old Road, one of four bay-windows. I was only a schoolgirl at time, my eldest brother is 84. His name is Frank Lassel. I have enjoyed thinking back."

Pete Burns, who lent me some wonderful old plans of the entire Friargate site, told me, when he was young he used to go up to the station after it had closed, around 1968. One day he went up there and he could smell gas (the station at that time was pretty much intact and the gas lighting was still in place). He thought nothing of it and that perhaps he had imagined it. About a week later part of the station burnt down.

The only gas lamp that is left now is outside the Engine House. It is not original, but it would be nice to think that it was replaced while the station was open. Until recently the Sugar Sheds still stood but unfortunately someone was fooling about there and was hurt, so the owner of the land demolished them.

During the late 1940s to the mid-1950s, **Mr Blundell** worked as an engineer's apprentice in the Engine House, where he had his own bench. He also recalls working in the Goods Depot itself. The station master at that time was residing in the living accommodation on the top floor (the rounded front of the building is three floors, rather than the two in the rest of the building). He was, remembers Mr Blundell, a 'funny old fellow', although unfortunately he cannot remember his name. The other two floors were taken up with office staff. He recalls that in the bad winter of 1947 all the hydraulic pipes from the Engine House to under the Goods Depot froze and replacing the burst pipes was a very big job.

There was a lift under the station, to the right of the stairs, that led up to the centre platform. The lift was powered by water that came from Mickleover Tunnel through over two miles of pipes. The Victorians who built the lift, he says, were very ingenious and used whatever resources were to hand. He also had to help mend the lift, as it needed a new piston cast. Under the arches was the candlemaker, Pybus, in the arch next to the one that led to the subway. The firm had been there a long time and one day he was shown how they made the candles, by pouring molten wax into moulds with wicks in. They made about 50 at a time.

In the 1950s he helped dismantle the hand crane that was on a plinth in the Goods Yard on Great Northern Road. He worked with a Harry Riggott, whose wife, Florence Riggott was Mayor of Derby in 1958. Mr Riggott was employed in the Loco Works.

Mr Blundell retired after working for the railways from a boy. One story he told me was particularly amusing but also illustrates why the Friargate line was losing money. Late one afternoon about 1955, a train trundled into the station pulling five carriages. It drew to a halt …and one little boy clutching a pile of books got off, presumably coming home from school. He must have felt like royalty!

Jack Wallis lives at Kirk Langley and worked at Friargate from 28 August 1950 until 1961. He is a fascinating man and his experiences alone could fill an entire book. He has great recall and tells many amusing and sometimes dramatic stories of Friargate. Let him tell, in his own words, of the sad loss of his friend Johnny Mannion. It illustrates the constant dangers that the workers faced and it is important that he is remembered as an important part of Friargate's history.

"It was a very misty, foggy morning, and terribly damp. Johnny had been working Fred Carey's job. Fred had been off bad with the 'flu for a fortnight but he reported right for work, so that meant Johnny going back firing. This is how it worked. We were both past-firemen, spare drivers, and Johnny was senior to me. I'd got that job, so Johnny took it off me …and I took another job on.

"We worked with Billy Onn, so it's got to be February 1956. I was firing for Billy. We were on the passenger trains — the loco was shut, so we were travelling to Nottingham.

"This Grantham driver came down and said: 'They've just told me I've killed one of your blokes!'

"I said: 'Where?'

"He said: 'Up at Breadsall somewhere there. They told me he was with a tamping machine.'

"I said: 'Christ, it's Johnny Mannion.'

"Then I said to Billy: 'That should've been my job. Johnny took it in there and out the way.'

"We think he'd had a row with his wife, I heard that it was his wedding anniversary as well. It went to court. Johnny was found 50 per cent responsible for his own death and the railways got blamed for the other 50per cent.

"The noise of the tamping machine was so bad that you couldn't stay with it while it was working — at least we couldn't, although the two drivers that operated it — Polish lads, I see them walking about town, I call them lads, they're getting on for 70 odd — they operated it everywhere.

"Johnny's widow got £1,000. In relation to what we were earning — about £7 a week with overtime — it would have been just over two years' earnings. It wasn't much because they found Johnny 50 per cent responsible exposing himself to danger."

I asked Jack if he would have put himself in the same position had he been working the machine. He said he couldn't answer that but from what he could see, the tamping machine was working on the up line and Johnny was killed on the down line because when Jack went to fetch the machine, that's where it was.

He said: "The police asked me: 'Where's your watch?' and I told them I hadn't got one. They asked how we knew when we had to get clear and I said that we had to guess the time. Perhaps Johnny had misjudged the time. We'd all brought our own watches. The loco drivers never got issued with a watch, only the guards. It was a sore point — why should the guard have it when we'd got to time the trains?"

I imagined Johnny standing on the down watching the tamping machine on the up, with his foot on the line. I asked about the gap between the lines. Jack continued: "The six foot? No, he'd have got killed in any case. He'd have got sucked in. It was horrible because he was chopped up just like a piece of meat."

I asked if it had been instantaneous. Jack said: "Christ, yes. I think all he'd have known would have been the vibration through his feet".

I asked about look-outs and Jack said: "No, they didn't have any. This was the point, this is why he got £1,000. I had to go and finish the job and I had to take it to Egginton and had a conductor from Egginton to Derby to take it round. I don't know whether I signed the road from Egginton to Derby, as you were never allowed on the roads unless you'd signed for it to say you were conversant with signalling, and the points and everything, and I know I fetched it down and I took it in and, funnily enough, when it came out again — I don't know if it was three or four weeks after I had to take it back to the same spot — this time they'd fitted a siren on it, a push button siren, and there was a look-out stationed on the off-side. Of course, I got all this information and took it straight to the union and said: 'Look this is what they have done. So if it was illegal before, they were negligent.' And that is why Johnny's widow got 50 per cent awarded but even if he'd have got the full £2,000 it was nothing, only four years' earnings. He'd only have been about 29, just starting off in married life."

The tragedy made the front page of the *Derby Evening Telegraph*, a small sad little piece that in no way did the dead railwayman justice. It read simply: 'Railman killed in Derby accident. A middle-aged Derby engine driver was decapitated in an accident on the main Derby to Nottingham railway line behind the premises of Thomas Hill and Co Ltd, scrap merchants, Mansfield Road Derby at 8.25 this morning. He was Mr John Mannion of 30 Chester Street, Derby, a married man with a two-year old daughter. He was taken to the DRI and was later identified. The facts have been reported to the Derby Borough Coroner Mr R.J.H.Cleaver.'

Even after all these years I feel it is important to stress that Johnny Mannion should not have been working in those conditions — the machine was too loud to operate safely without look-outs, and none were posted. His employers were largely to blame for his needless death.

We got talking, inevitably perhaps, about suicides because this is something that train drivers have always had to cope with. Jack talked about the time he fired for a man called Poacher. As luck would have it, Jack was on holiday when this particular tragedy occurred. Poacher was going to Sheffield or Leeds with an express train. There was this chap, who Jack thinks was a retired miner suffering from an industrial disease. He took his dog in his arms and stepped out in front of the train. Poacher said he looked him straight in the eyes.

Jack said: "The express was going about 70 miles an hour and the stopping distance of a steam express was about two miles — on the old vacuum brakes it was a minute per mile and it took three-quarters of a minute for the brakes to whack through the length of the train. With today's air brakes it is a lot quicker, though of course, it's still too late with three to four hundred tons bearing down on anyone in the way."

Jack continued: "There was another fellow who worked in the gang, who got bowled over by a train but he was crippled. It depends how the train hits you. If you think of a loco, the front end of that buffer beam, if that hits you on the back of the head — you have had it."

Another of Jack's stories concerns the time before he worked on the Friargate line, but was travelling home on leave from the army on a Friargate train.

"It was Easter 1949 and coming home on leave we ran into six horses. They were on the main line and the train hit them. The impact was such that they broke the steel pipe that comes up with the vacuum pack for the brakes. They flattened that straight out, so the brakes went on instantly. One horse went underneath the engine and forced itself up past the ash vat. Of course, it was dead by then. Another got its head inside the piston. The rest got chopped up — the one that went under the train got roasted under the ash van,– and one had burst the steel pipe and actually bent the buffer beam. They managed to drag the train off, pulled the strings in the carriages so the brakes were off, dragged it to the nearest station and waited for another engine to take over and work it.

"One day at Spondon, we had to go out one day with a chap called George. A flock of sheep had got on to the tracks and been hit by a train."

I said jokingly: "Roast Lamb that day then? You didn't eat any of them ...did you?"

"Bloody true I did. This driver couldn't touch it, turned him right off,. But it made no difference to me — meat's meat. I had my share of it. It would only have been dumped at the slaughter house. Once they're dead, that's it"

About 40-50 sheep had been hit and the sight probably turned the other driver into a vegetarian for life.

One last story of Jack's days at Friargate is about when he came down from Ambergate very early one morning to find the railway covered in white packets, which turned out to contain Park Drive cigarettes.

"They must have fallen out of a goods train. Anyway we picked up as many as we could and took them to the local police station. All we took was a couple of packets because we did not have a smoke on us. The rest, as no duty had been paid on them, had to be burned."

Jack said finally: "If only you could capture the spirit of the Friargate men, the railroad, the friendships that were made. Perhaps things just look better looking back, but I loved my job and my days at Friargate. I was a lucky man".

Robin Beck worked as a clerk at Friargate Station from the age of 15. Among the people he remembered were the station master Sid Woodward, chief clerk Stan Callard, clerks Mick Weaver and Dick Ravensdale, drivers (past firemen) Billy Onn, Percy Sims, Bram Hunt, George Woodings, Benny Ault and Alf Otter, guards Brian Atkins, Jimmy Morrell, Walter Salisbury and Harry Botham, foremen George Rushby and Len Eyre, shunters Tommy Moorley and Ali, porters Dave Tristram, Sid Jones, Mohammed Ahkbar and Mohammed Malik, carriage cleaner Mrs Ault and British Transport Police officers Geoff Colby and Gordon England.

He told me, for all you people out there who bought tickets for that last train in 1964, it was Robin Beck who sold them to you, for he was the last clerk on duty that day.

I asked him about the water lift which was located on the centre platform. It was powered, he believes, by water from St Mary's Wharf. Sid Jones, the man who ran the lift, was only small and to get the lift going the piston had to be struck with a large hammer. Sid Jones had difficulty reaching and there would be a lot swearing before he got it going. Apparently it made a hell of a noise when it was working. Now, of course, the area is so overgrown that one can find no trace of the lift.

The drivers had a separate little room underneath the arches, cold and damp and, of course, gas lit. Robin had to go in to deliver messages.

He recalls: "Percy Sims must have been about the oldest. In fact, I think he retired from Friargate. Bram Hunt and George Woodings would have been the youngest. Walter Salisbury was actually over age. He was about 70 but they let you carry on in those days. Sadly one chap, Stan Callard, the chief clerk, had a heart attack and died on Friargate Station. He'd been rushing to work and just collapsed. While I worked there the station master, Sid Woodward, also died and we had a lot of relief station masters from then."

He recalls his first day being shown round by the chief clerk, the high ceilings of the offices, and how Malik commented on how small he was: "He thought I was a jockey. I was the smallest in class when I left school, but I soon shot up a bit when I started work."

I asked if the Fish Docks were still being used when he was there. He remembers the trains from Hull and Grimsby coming in and how afterwards the docks had to be swilled down. Fish from Grimsby was under the control of the Fish Merchants' Association and one of their representatives would come down early in the morning to check that the fish had arrived fresh and that all the weigh tickets were in place. Two drivers would arrive about 6am to collect the fish, to deliver it to the Fish Market, Kingsway Hospital and Roome's of Sadler Gate. One was called Harry Baker, the other Frank Thomas.

Says Robin: "They would load up and Frank was soon away. But Harry Baker? Well, time had no meaning to Harry! Up on the Fish Dock was a little hut, and inside was a chap, a kind of security guard, who would sit there all day. He had a little coal-burning stove which he kept going all day and the temperature in there was about 100 degrees, it would hit you as you walked in. Harry would go in about 8.30am and chat to this guy for two to three hours, drinking tea, when, of course, he should have been delivering the fish!"

Robin also remembers the huge parcel trains: "One used to come in with boxes and boxes of flowers from Spalding and that area. The porters would have to start to unload around 3.30am. Vans used to come during the day to collect the parcels and any that were left would be stored overnight in the Parcel Office. This was used as a bit of a dumping ground for rubbish and papers. One morning when I got to work I saw all up the path what I thought was fish, but when I got closer I saw it was wet paper. The Parcel Office had caught fire during the night. They thought that the last person to leave had chucked a cigarette away into all this rubbish and that is what started it.

"The Goods Depot used to store flour from one of the nearby mills, which I think was in Manchester Street. Also, there was a catalogue office based upstairs before it all moved to London Road. There were a lot of girls and machines up there. Horses would also come through the station, with proper vans with sleeping accommodation for the groom. Volkswagon cars used to come in from the ferry at Ramsgate, on big flat trucks. I learnt to drive at Friargate, sometimes the drivers would let you have a go. When the train carrying all the chocolate from Cadburys came in, it would spend the night in the siding. The British Transport Police would keep their eyes on it. Imagine, a train full of chocolate!

"In the Ticket Office was a coke-burning stove. And, of course, there was always plenty of fuel around. The toilet was the other side of the Booking Hall, sort of behind the arches, you wouldn't know it was there. We also sold tickets so that people could park their cars underneath the arches, on the Booking Hall side. There was also a Banana Warehouse in one of the arches as the temperature was just right. You should have seen some of the creepy spiders and things that used to come in with the bananas!

"At the end of the bridge, the Agard Street side, was a huge signal. It was one of the porter's jobs to fill the oil lamps. One summer's night one of the porters offered me the chance to go up and refill the lamps. The signal itself was quite high, and added to the height of the bridge — well it was very high! In fact, you don't realise just how high it is until you were up there.

"Up on the platform we had trouble with rats. When they cleaned out the carriages they just used to sweep them out and there was this big mound of rubble and all sorts. In summer, when it was hot, this mound used to move with rats!

"On a Sunday you had to work three turns, I wouldn't bother going home. I'd stay and help out where I could. It wasn't that busy during the winter but the parcel traffic was much the same.

"You had your regular customers all year round and that kept it going. Of course, summer made up for the slow winter. Then it was really busy. I can remember people queuing up right under the bridge on Friargate."

We got talking about accidents, which mercifully were rare, Robin did, however, remember one incident when he took a call from the control: "They told me: 'We think the train coming in has hit somebody on the line — can you get someone to go and see if their are any traces.' Well I didn't think. I went up there with one of the foremen and we looked all round the engine and carriages but we could see no sign of anything. It turned out it was the other train out of Nottingham on the other line that hit someone."

One of his duties was to pay out the wages: "In those days I used to go up to the Post Office on Uttoxeter Old Road and buy National Insurance stamps. Different people paid for different stamps. The wages were all done by hand and I had to work out what each person was owed. I used to go most days on my bike to the bank on the Market Place, the National and Provincial, I think it's Nat West now. In those days you didn't have to worry about carrying money round in your saddle bag. In the Ticket Office there was racks and racks of pre-printed tickets, some were so old they were yellow and crumbling. Each year we used to sell one ticket to Fort William, either to Mr or Mrs Strutt. That's where Mr Strutt went missing — they never found him."

Robin can remember Friargate as if it was yesterday, and he thoroughly enjoyed his time there. Of course, in those days, when you finished one job you had no trouble finding another, and from Friargate he moved on to Midland Road, but that, as they say, is another story.

During the early 1950s my own great-grandmother travelled on one of these trains, non-corridor, in a no smoking compartment, having to puff the smoke out of the window, so as not to offend the other passengers.

My father can remember during the middle 1950s taking my mother to Skegness, a very grand thing to do in the post-war years.

It seems that everyone over 50 can remember the Friargate line, not with the complaints that are common when discussing British Rail, but with much affection. Les Sayers described it really well — as a 'romantic line'. Dick Clegg said that he would rather travel on this line to Nottingham, than go from the Midland Station, and that the steep incline to Breadsall added to the fun.

The Last Train Leaving ...

An article in the *Derby Evening Telegraph* of 27 August 1964 signalled the demise of the station: 'The laconic announcement of changes in passenger train services from 7 September issued by British Railways, reminds those who have a sentimental interest in the Midlands that their opportunities to travel on these lines are to end.

'The lines are the Derby Friargate to Nottingham, (Victoria) and the Burton to Leicester (London Road), both of which in their heyday were busy services. Officially the service ends at midnight on Sunday, 6 September 1964, but as there are no Sunday trains, the last train on Saturday evening will mark the end of the service. The Derby Friargate line was opened by the Great Northern Railways to link Derby with Nottingham (Midland) then operated by the Midland Railway Co in 1878. It was not until 1900 that GNR combined with the Great Central Railway Co to link Friargate with Nottingham Victoria. For those who wish to take a sentimental last journey over the line, the last train leaves from Derby at 10.10pm and arrives Nottingham at 10.45pm.'

On 11 September 1964, the *Derbyshire Advertiser* reported: 'Last Saturday was closing day for many railway passengers services in Britain. Among them the Friargate-Nottingham service which has operated from Derby for nearly a hundred years. It was a dark wet night, when I went to Friargate to catch the 10.10, the last train ever to leave Friargate. Thoughtfully, British Railways had laid on a number of extra coaches for this occasion and many of these were filled with enthusiasts — perhaps mourners would be a more appropriate word — anxious to pay respect to a service to which we felt we owed something over the years but had left it too late. Some carried bells which rang out into the darkness from carriage windows, others brought pistols which they fired intermittently as the train sped towards its last stopping place. The fireman kept his whistle blowing continuously as if trying to use up any surplus steam before reaching Nottingham. I cannot help wondering how it came about that this line has remained open to passengers for so long. The few people who used it could hardly have paid for the upkeep of one train, let alone six or seven in each direction. For twenty years at least the service must have been a dead loss to British Railways. Somehow the whole of the surroundings were in keeping with Victorian austerity which saw the Friargate line into being. The gas lighting on the station, the old horse-cab stands, even the locomotive was a real vintage specimen as if specially recruited for a last journey. At Nottingham Victoria the train emptied itself and many made their way towards the driver who smilingly autographed tickets which the purchasers (no doubt strictly against the rules) kept as souvenirs.'

Friargate Station touched the lives of many people, both workers and the travellers. Even today over 30 years since it closed, people are still fascinated with the station's past. I hope this book continues to keep the memory of Friargate alive.

This shows Short Street before it was demolished by the GNR. This view from 1872, which shows how Agard Street was connected to Friargate, has disappeared. Replaced on one side by arches, the building at the top of the street is dated 1780 so is original (and all that is left of this view which framed the entrance to Short Street). The Lord Hill (centre) was one of many public houses demolished by the GNR. The street was, according to the Town Council, one of many that would not be missed. They even showed Friargate in a poor light to help get the project through Parliament. Many of the council had much to gain, as they owned property and industrial premises in the areas that the GNR needed to purchase. It was said that one street, Willow Row, in particular was the town's most notorious slum district. Back-to-back houses were crammed tightly together with dirty courts and alleyways, a focal point for petty crime and prostitution. It has to be said for all the underhand dealings, the railway did do a lot of good for Derby, bringing trade in and out of the town. It was also much more convenient than Midland Road for the public and the old established mills and foundries, as it was closer to the town centre and would give rail access for the industrial part of Friargate. Many firms would benefit from the GNR. It is ironic that now Midland Road is our main station, although Friargate would still be more conveniently placed, even in the age of the car.

Friargate looking towards the side where the Tram Depot was situated to the right of the shops in this photograph. The buildings are 18th-century, so the very end one must be from the corner of Short Street. (see previous illustration). *B.Bourne.*

Close up of the building at the corner of the former Short Street. *S.Bourne.*

Both these photographs look towards Friargate Bridge. Note the pointed roof on the right-hand photograph corresponds with that of the building on the first illustration. *B.Bourne.*

January 1996 and early on a Saturday morning the site, now a car park, is empty. The tram lines, the cobbles and one lone arch (out of shot to the right) are all that is left. You can see the faint line that the arches took along the right-hand side of the photograph. *S.Bourne.*

Taken from the station side from the top of the Cob Shop, this view shows the bridge bricked-off at the end and leading nowhere. In the background you can just see the car park where the arches stood. On the horizon is one of the old mills. *S.Bourne.*

Taken in the early 1980s, this shows the inside of one of the arches on the Agard Street side of the station, where the Tram Depot once stood. Now empty before demolition and soon to be gone forever. *Alf Bousie.*

Shown in the 1980s before the arches on the Agard Street side were demolished, this is where Short Street once stood, to be replaced by the arches and the Tramway Yard. These photographs show before and afterwards. It is surprising that the cobbles and what is left of the tram lines survive. It is now a car park. *Steve Higgins.*

The arches on the station side. In the distance can be seen the entrance to the subway. This went to the centre platform. Under the original plans it would have gone to the first platform where all the main station buildings would have been. This first platform was eventually the Fish Docks. On 15 September 1980 the *Derby Evening Telegraph* reported that: 'Firms occupying the arches were declared safe after the recent collapse of one of the arches, which had been used as a workshop. Firms have lost trade because of groundless fears by customers. Mr Steve Nightingale, Auto Repairs, based in one of the six archways between Friargate bridge and Agard Street [now demolished] says he has lost money since the collapse of the arches beneath the old station.' The article goes on to quote him:

"Regular customers have been ringing me at home to see if I'm still in business because they have heard of other firms moving out." He pointed out that his arch was part of a stretch that was completely separate from the arches that were at the centre of the collapse. "Our arch supports Friargate Bridge so if there were any structural failure it would affect the bridge itself." If his business supported the bridge, the collapse must have been on the station side, so why was the Agard Street side knocked down? Perhaps so many firms went under, and in the photograph on the following page it looks pretty derelict. It is a pity the arches were not preserved as they were an important feature of the bridge. On this side the arch that collapsed is used to store old doors ready for stripping, and a lot of rubble from the collapse. *J.Coker.*

Taken from the arches on the station side, this view looks towards the bridge. There is a line of cobbles and what looks like an old tram line, turned on its side. The Victorians never wasted anything and would utilise any spare materials they had to hand. In the background, (top right) stands the District Engineers house. *J.Coker.*

Showing the entrance to the station from an original photograph c.1956 British Rail (OPC).

March 1996. The entrance is still intact, Mike Cordon, who has been there since the early 1960s, still has his car lot there. The whole scene is very little changed.

Taken in the 1980s before the Booking Office was demolished and afterwards. Note in the left-hand picture the old noticeboard on the left-hand wall. The entrance to the subway can be seen in the picture, right. The old crimson doors have been replaced with new ones. In both pictures the old cobbled road can still be seen. *Steve Higgins.*

Inside the main entrance to the Booking Hall, still intact and serving a useful purpose as a car lot.

Through the main booking hall, the large arch leads into the subway that led travellers on to the centre platform.

The subway looking to the island platform *c.*1956 British Rail photograph. (OPC), and *right,* the same view today, the subway has been blocked off and the stairs on the other side have been filled with rubble.

This photograph was taken in the early 1980s, from the subway before it was filled in with rubble. The stairs are intact but overgrown. *Steve Higgins.* The photograph below shows the subway filled in and extended by a Perspex roof. As seen in the photograph top right, it has been bricked off and the area is used to jack up cars. *J.Coker.*

This would have been the main entrance. Until the money ran out and plans had to be altered, this would have led to the first platform which would have had buildings covered with a canopy. In fact all the platforms were to have had covered buildings and were planned to be much grander than things turned out. In the end it was mainly used for loading goods and was used as a Fish Dock. It was also used as an Excursion Platform.

The arches a little further along. Under the station the sub-structure was very extensive and housed many businesses. One part was also stables used to deliver and collect goods around Derby. There was also a porters' room. There were ten arches and these were inter-linked by cartways, the fifth arch incorporating the passenger subway. Again, because it had been partially completed under a more ambitious plan, the passageway continued right under the station and came out on the south side to an overgrown slope. *J.Coker.*

Walking up to the subway entrance from the arches, a doorway is hidden by doors and scrap wood. Under the original plans this would have been the main entrance. At the very end of the arches is a doorway *(shown pictured right)* leading to another unknown room. It could lead into the arches, it could have been a firm's entrance. *J.Coker.*

Part of the generous approach road to the station from Stafford Street that became vacant when the GNR had to alter its plans. This was eventually let to a firm of timber and slate merchants, Smart & Elsom, who erected these buildings. *J.Coker.*

Another building that was part of Smart & Elsom. *J.Coker.*

June 1996. Two photographs of the Engine House with its Italianate tower, now used by a pine workshop. The roof is in need of repair and the interior of the building is unrecognisable. A gas lamp minus its fittings stands outside. There was a lamp in this location and although this is not original GNER, it would be nice to think that it was replaced when the station was open. When in use the Engine House supplied all the hydraulic power for the capstans, cranes and hoists in the Goods Depot. It also provided power for the goods lift at the station. *B Bourne*.

Two further views of the Engine House, this time taken from the other side where the roof looks intact. *B.Bourne.*

Under the original plans the main entrance would have faced Stafford Street instead of Friargate. The approach roads, platforms and sub-structures had already been constructed before the GNR had to cut costs and do away with the roof that would have covered all the platforms and the main buildings. In the end the station was completed with buildings on the centre platform only. The approach road is still there, partly cobbled. This picture, taken in the 1980s, shows old British Rail posters. The gate is very fragile but still in its original colour. *Steve Higgins.*

The cobbled approach road in Stafford Street in June 1996. As previously stated this would have been the main entrance. The small wicket gate has been repaired and gone is any trace of the BR notices. The building to the right is now part of Henry Boot training.

Part of the Meter House and Weigh Office. The window is bricked-up and the metal door doesn't quite fit but the roof is intact. The building to the right has been demolished.

The entrance to the subway, off Great Northern Road, that leads under the Goods Depot. Later used by Thomas & Bee Woodcraft Ltd and as car workshops etc, and partitioned off for different businesses, it is now very run down and dark, but for all that pretty much intact. *J.Coker.*

J39 heading past Derby East Signal Box in August 1959. The Goods Depot is in the background. Note the telegraph pole at the side of the Signal Box. *G.A.Yeomans.*

Almost the same view, but very overgrown. If you go too far back you lose the Goods Depot behind the mound, part of which used to be the Derby East Signal Box. Note the telegraph pole still in place. In the rubble of the mound is a lot of wood painted crimson and cream (LNER colours), a large sash window and some wooden running boards which could be part of the Signal Box or the station itself. *J.Coker.*

Around 1968, close to the Sugar Sheds. The piles of lifted rails are ready for the scrap trains. Perhaps the lone wagon in the background is to be used for that very purpose. *Alf Bousie.*

Derby East Signal Box photographed around 1966-68. Note the footbridge bottom left, wagons to the right. The area is still active but has the air of neglect about it. *Alf Bousie.*

Familiar view of Friargate Station in 1965, now closed but still intact. *Alf Henshaw.*

Taken 1968 from the footbridge, this photograph shows all the main buildings are still there including the Sugar and Goods Sheds. In the middle right is the Engine House. *Alf Bousie.*

The Goods Depot in 1968. Note that one of the lines has been lifted and left in piles ready for collection. *Alf Bousie*.

An unusual view of the Derby East Signal Box in 1968, taken from some lock-up garages on South Street, looking up the embankment. Like the Signal Box, the garages are long gone, replaced with a small block of flats. *Alf Bousie*.

View of Derby East Signal Box 1970. The Goods Depot can be seen to the side and the rails are still in place. *Steve Higgins.*

The mound near the Goods Depot that is all that remains of Derby East Signal Box. Note at the bottom right of the mound is a small wall with steel pins sticking out. This could be part of the lower part of the Signal Box. *J.Coker.*

General rubble from the site of the Derby East Signal Box. It has all been pushed forward by the bulldozers. The windows could be from anywhere. *B.Bourne.*

Solid concrete with supporting metal rods. This could be part of the base of the Signal Box.

Derby Friargate in 1950, taken from the Fish Dock looking towards the bridge. Derby Cathedral and St Alkmund's Church (now demolished) are in the background. The gas lamps are a major feature but the whole place looks a little neglected and the platform in the foreground looks very rough. *Alan Rimmer.*

Almost the same view as on the previous page. Note the spire of St Alkmund's has been shortened. This photograph, taken in 1959, shows the platforms in better condition. *G.A. Yeomans.*

Derby Friargate in 1963-64. A train pulls into station past the old Fish Docks. Note the bus in the background and the lone traveller, hands in pockets. *Alf Bousie.*

Unknown train taking on water in 1964. No staged poses here, everyone is busy doing their jobs. This photograph was taken on the centre platform opposite the Station Inspector's office. *Alf Bousie.*

The water crane situated on the centre platform outside the Station Inspector's office in 1965. The site is becoming very overgrown. *Alf Henshaw.*

In 1965 the trimmed back canopy and the buildings look very worn and neglected. The station had been closed for almost a year when this photograph was taken. The water crane can just be seen in the distance. *Alf Henshaw.*

Looking from the centre platform towards the Goods Depot in August 1959. Note the recess in the outer walling where, under the original plans, the entrance to the subway would have been. *G.A.Yeomans.*

This view taken in June 1996 is also from the centre platform but further down. It is so overgrown that if you stand in the spot from where the original photograph was taken, you lose the Goods Depot completely. *B.Bourne.*

Overgrown in 1996. This photograph is taken from where the tracks would have been. Only the platforms remain and the only other landmark is the house in the background. *J.Coker.*

The same view as the previous one, although from a little further up towards the bridge, standing on the centre platform, roughly where the Station Inspector's office was situated. *B.Bourne.*

The mid-1950s looking towards the Derby East Signal Box. The Goods Depot is on the left and the large lattice signal is more or less centre. *G.A.Yeomans.*

A close-up of what is left of the signal. It was only found by accident when the author's husband fell over it! *B.Bourne.*

A close up of the signal on the down side, as seen in the previous photograph. Drawing by Nicholas Coker Bourne from the original photograph by Alan Rimmer. The signal denotes 'Proceed with caution' and is dated from the 1950s.

Train taking on water in 1954, from one of the two water cranes. The other was just before the bridge. *G.A. Yeomans.*

More-or-less the same view as the previous photograph but from a little further down the platform. The gas lights can be seen and the station looks in good condition. *G.A. Yeomans.*

Friargate Station about 1954, before the station was painted, looking towards the Goods Depot. *G.A. Yeomans.*

Friargate in August 1959, after the station had been painted. The same view, but a little closer. The sign has been changed to Derby Friargate and flowers have been planted to brighten up the station. *G.A. Yeomans.*

Friargate in 1963 and steam meets diesel. Note the station in the background, the canopy has been trimmed back to save on maintenance. *Ken Cook.*

D.3 2123 at
Friargate in April
1949. *Alan Rimmer.*

J6 number unknown in the up Excursion Platform. The imposing Royal School for the Deaf, opened in 1894 and demolished to be replaced by modern flats in 1974, is in the background. The photograph is before 1958 because the station has yet to be repainted. *Alan Rimmer.*

D2 4-4-0 arriving at Friargate, on to the centre platform. Again pre-1958. *Alan Rimmer.*

RCTS 'The Mercian' at Friargate on 2 June 1957, photographed by G.A.Yeomans. Note the water crane. To the left of this is the small building on the original plans dated 1880 and corrected in 1903. It was the Station Inspector's office. Next to that was a shunter's hut. From this there was then the gentlemens' toilet, then the main station buildings of General Waiting Room, Ladies' Waiting Room 2nd class, and at the top of the subway stairs the famous Refreshment Room. Then came the subway entrance. In 1993, when the picture below was taken by Rob Passey, the subway was still not blocked off. The next block of buildings walking towards the bridge were Ladies' Waiting Room 1st class, the water lift in the Waiting Room itself, Gents Waiting Room 1st class and lastly a small office. There was another water crane just before the bridge.

A close up view of what is left of the water crane as shown in the previous photographs, taken in the 1980s. *Steve Higgins*.

This photograph, taken in 1996, shows all that is left today. The pipes are still in the hole where the tree is growing but what little remained has gone. *J.Coker.*

The roof on top of the Cob Shop, quite tidy compared with the rest of the station. *J.Coker.*

One of the last telegraph poles on the station itself, still more or less intact in 1996. *J.Coker.*

Derby Friargate pictured on 23 April 1949. 4-4-0 D2 class No 2190 with the up train to Grantham. Note the water crane (there were two on the station itself), and lattice gantry signal on the bridge. *Alan Rimmer.*

The same view as seen on the previous page, just before the bridge, taken in the 1980s. There is no sign of the water crane, but the supports to the station sign can still be seen.
Steve Higgins.

Friargate on 23 April 1949. B1 No 1227, on up freight, coming from the station on to the bridge. *Alan Rimmer.*

Friargate Bridge today. The rails have gone but the rest is intact. Threatened with demolition in 1973, for an extension to the inner ring road – which as yet remains to be built – and repainted in 1978, it is now listed Grade II. The bridge is still technically under threat and the planned road, which would have gone above and within the bridge, would have had a devastating effect upon Friargate Conservation Area.

Friargate Bridge, intact apart from the rails. Vandals have been active as usual, but otherwise it is nicely preserved. The expresses used to make the arches rattle.

Taking on water just before Friargate bridge around 1963. *Ken Cook*.

This 1984 photograph was taken from a similar position to the previous one, and before the bridge was blocked off. *Rob Passey*.

A train crosses Friargate Bridge around 1950. Note the war time black-out markings. *Alan Rimmer.*

Looking down Friargate in 1993. The cobbles are from the approach road to the Booking Hall, now a car sales business. *Rob Passey.*

An unusual view of Friargate Bridge, taken in July 1996 from the fire escape across the road on the Agard Street side. *J.Coker.*

This 1996 photograph was taken from the opposite side of the bridge, looking up Friargate. The cobbles are part of the approach road to the arches. *J.Coker.*

The Goods Depot from the outside. Although this listed building looks intact, it is more or less derelict on the inside.

There are precious few red telephone boxes anywhere in England these days but one has survived in the conservation area of Friargate. Such a box has stood on this site and appeared on all old views of Friargate since the 1940s. *J.Coker.*

Under the bridge is this nameplate. Handyside had started work in Derby in 1848 when they moved into an existing ironworks on the east side of Duke Street. By the 1890s Handyside was employing 1,200 men, a big increase from 30 years before when their workforce numbered 350. On 28 September 1910, they went into voluntary liquidation, starting up again in 1915 but on a much smaller scale. *B.Bourne.*

The front of the Goods Depot, which was divided into three storeys instead of two as in the rest of the building. There was a top-floor residence for the Goods Manager, the rest being used as goods offices. After nationalisation, the second and third floors were used by the BR Chief of Supplies and Contracts Officer and his staff. Here they printed parts of the railway catalogues for the whole network. They had been housed previously near Midland Road Station. The building was curved at the front and the whole structure made impressive because under the original plans it would have been visible from the front by the public It was also to have had a tower topped by a conical roof, with a weather-vane, and also a double-faced clock, but none of this came to pass.

Inside the rounded front of the building, showing what is left and safely accessible at the time this photograph was taken. *B.Bourne.*

Looking straight up to the glass-topped roof, one flight of stairs partially collapsed. *B.Bourne.*

On the top left of the building was the Fire Brigade Station, attached to the Goods Depot. *S.Bourne.*

A view of the hoist. Still in the LNER colours of cream and crimson, it is the only one to survive on the Goods Depot. *B.Bourne.*

Viewed from the Engine House side, the tracks terminated here. Originally there were hoists spaced all along the Goods Depot. The wooden door is intact, complete with small raised platform. This photograph was taken in 1993. *Rob Passey.*

Where the wooden door once stood, a grain chute is still in place. Inside are remains of the loading platforms. This photograph was taken in 1996, just before the doorway was bricked up. Note the pile of bricks ready for the job in the foreground. *J.Coker.*

The windows on the lower left-hand side of the Goods Depot, behind which was the Hose Room. The Goods Depot had its own Fire Station attached to the outside of the warehouse. The doorway in the centre of the picture was access for road vehicles. *J.Coker.*

On the side of the Goods Depot, was this fire bucket stand, the buckets long gone but the brackets surviving when this photograph was taken in the 1980s. *Steve Higgins.*

This entrance was for road vehicle access, the bricked-up doorway to the right led into the offices. Note the big wooden doors to the Goods Depot. *J.Coker.*

Those massive wooden doors *(pictured overleaf)* pictured from the inside. *J.Coker.*

Stairs leading to the stores underneath the Goods Depot. Very steep, they were used to roll barrels of goods down into the stores or hauled up to the station to be loaded on to the trains. *B.Bourne.*

The back of the Goods Depot. The doorways are almost completely bricked up. The small building to the right was a weigh office. *J.Coker.*

The remains of the base of the crane which was close to the Goods Depot. *J.Coker.*

View from the back of the Goods Depot towards the front. *B.Bourne.*

Side view from the back to the rounded front of the building. Along its top edge were the words 'LNER Goods Depot'. Since the railways closure it has been used by a variety of firms. *B.Bourne.*

A picture taken from the back of the building. Note the arched doorway to the right. Also the top of the ornate pillar. It is interesting to recall that during its time as an LNER Goods Depot, this building was lit entirely by gas.

The now partially bricked-up entrance to the Goods Depot. The floor of the warehouse is wooden and note the top-middle square walkway. No floors to the upper offices can be seen.

From the front of the building. Note the platform level can still be seen.

Arched doorway leading to an office complete with fireplace. The wooden staircase far top right leads to what was apparently a foreman's office, again with fireplace. The floor in this office is very unsafe.

In 1987 the spiral
staircase is still
attached, leading
to the upper floor
of the Goods
Depot. *Alf Bousie*.

Taken at the same time as the previous one, this photograph shows the upper floor very unsafe. What is
left of partitions for the various offices which occupied this floor can be seen. *Alf Bousie*.

The back of the Goods Depot showing the spiral staircase. The platform is not original. Note the bricked-up doorway on the right-hand side which once led to a small outbuilding. There is an arched window to the left and part of the upper storey floor can be seen.

The Sugar Shed can just be seen in this 1993 photograph. *Rob Passey.*

By 1996, the site had been cleared. Now only a vague outline of the Sugar Shed foundations can be seen. *B. Bourne.*

The Sugar Shed seen from the back of the Goods Depot in 1993. It is very overgrown and strewn with rubble from another demolished building. *Rob Passey.*

The back of the Goods Depot in 1993. The Weigh Office still stands, as do most of the original wooden doors. *Rob Passey.*

The Sugar Shed during the 1980s. The roof is in a poor state of repair but the line of the tracks outside the building can just be seen. *Steve Higgins.*

A 1993 photograph of the Sugar Shed, by now being used as workshops. Rob Passey, who took the picture, used to go there to practice with his band. Note the outside wall has been painted and metal fencing has been erected.

Looking towards the station, the line of the tracks is clearly visible. These pictures show the plant-life. In summer it is a very attractive site. It should be preserved as it is, if nothing else, something of a nature reserve these days. *S.Bourne.*

Looking towards the Goods Depot a little further down the line towards the Derby West Signal Box. Note how the footpath still follows the line of the tracks. *S.Bourne.*

One of the sleepers which once held the rails. Most have been ripped up with the rails but a few isolated ones still exist. *S.Bourne.*

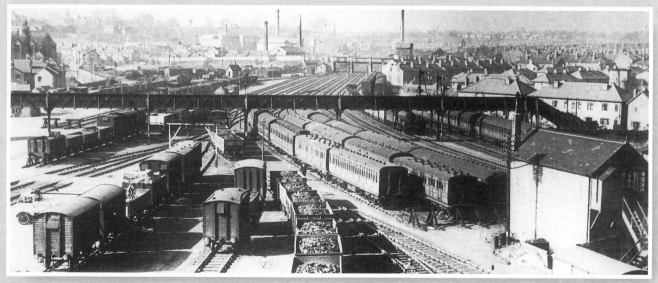

Derby Friargate Goods Yard in the 1940s, looking west towards Slack Lane. Derby East Signal Box is on the right. The footbridge leads to Great Northern Road to the left, and Ponsonby Terrace to the right. The bridge which still carries Uttoxeter Old Road over the route of the line is in the middle-distance.

This photograph looks back towards Friargate, from the bridge carrying the road off Slack Lane to the former Rowditch brickyards. The building to the right is now Hazelwood Foods offices.   *B.Bourne.*

A similar viewpoint in 1966, taken from beneath the bridge as a goods train passes the factory and siding of Burrows & Sturgess. The building (right) was then part of Pelapone Ltd.   *Jack Southall*

J6 64273 coming off Loco Depot at Slack Lane in January 1951. Note the footbridge in the background. *Alan Rimmer.*

Granville Street severed by the GNR. One can see the shadows of where the other house joined. The line of the tracks is clearly visible (bottom left). *S.Bourne.*

As far as one can go on this footpath from the station. In the central background College Primary School, which closed in late 1996. *S.Bourne.*

A5 4.6.2T 69805 at Friargate around 1954. *Alan Rimmer.*

Friargate Station in 1963. A very hazy Derby East Signal Box is in the background to the far left of the photograph. *Ken Cook.*

J1 65007 in Derby Friargate Yard in the 1950s. Note the discarded oil-can in the foreground. *Alan Rimmer.*

J6 65023 and V2 60930 at Slack Lane Depot in the 1950s. *Alan Rimmer.*

Friargate with A5 No 69805 standing in up Excursion Platform. *Alan Rimmer.*

Friargate with D3 4-4-0 2140 in the up Excursion Platform in April 1949. *Alan Rimmer.*

J6 at Slack Lane in the 1950s. Note the Coaling Stage-Tank House in the background. Under the canopy attached to the Tank House is another water crane, one of many staged along the tracks. *Alan Rimmer.*

Looking west in August 1959. Derby West Signal Box is in the foreground, the Tank House on the right. In the right middle-distance Shelton Terrace runs off Slack Lane down to the tracks. *G.A. Yeomans.*

N1 69457 at Slack Lane Loco Depot in 1954. Friargate Shed is in the background. *Alan Rimmer.*

Derby Slack Lane, showing J5 0-6-0 No 65498, built at Doncaster in 1909 as GNR class J22 No 39, which when withdrawn in 1955 was one of the last two members. The shed was gas-lit until it closed. *Alan Rimmer.*

Slack Lane, Derby outside the Engine Shed, around 1954 when it was very dilapidated. Friargate Shed, as it was known, closed in 1955. *Alan Rimmer.*

J2 0-6-0 65019. Again around 1954, before the shed finally closed. *Alan Rimmer.*

J1 0-6-0 at Slack Lane. Friargate Shed is in the background. Note the off license in the background.
Alan Rimmer.

The same shop on the corner of Brough Street in 1996. If you look closely you can just see Strettons Fine Ales sign on the wall by the door. The top sign has been painted out.
B.Bourne.

Friargate Shed, a recent view taken from Slack Lane when the site was owned by E.A.West of Parcel Terrace. The shed was closed in 1955 due, it was claimed, to the poor condition of the roof. The building was still in use 40 years later – all it needed was a new roof! Some of the walls inside the building are 2ft thick and to say it is solidly built would be an understatement. Inside it is pretty much intact, although it has been partitioned off for the various processes. On being shown around by Bill Worton and Nick Hawley, I saw there was more to this building than I thought – for a start the size. From the road it is impossible to appreciate how large it is. There are also some interesting features such as fireplaces. Open fires kept the workers warm in winter – after all there was no shortage of coal. The original roof, or what was left of it, was still there, under the new one. The main drain runs under the shed and occasionally it floods. As Nick Hawley pointed out, we were below street level. He showed me a line on the wall that marks the street level.

As you will see from the following pictures there is a lot left. There are small buildings attached to the shed which I will describe later. Although it is not a handsome building, considering the history of it, it would be a shame if it vanished like most of Friargate Station. The lines were never dug up, just concreted over, and in places they are beginning to show through again. At the back of the building the original roadway is still there, covered with soil and debris.

The site is under threat. E.A.West relocated to Grimsby in March 1998 with the site scheduled to be flattened, and although Lakes, the firm next to them, may take over part of the site, what of Friargate Shed? It has managed to survive the station's closure, but may not be so lucky next time. It could be turned into something really useful and with a little imagination it would make an ideal museum to Friargate Station. *B.Bourne.*

Friargate Shed, a photograph taken from what was the Goods Yard. The shed originally had four tracks and could accommodate over eight engines. The first building was originally a sand oven, the next one was a fireman's room and an office (taken from the plan of the station dated 1880, and corrected in 1903). E.A.West, who owned the site until 1998, kindly let me see round the building, Mr Wates told me the firm was started by two sisters, Elisa and Ann, in 1835. *B.Bourne.*

Under the new roof, the supports for the old one remain. Inside this is a deceptively large building, but many of the original features survive. *B.Bourne.*

Inside the shed. Note the old rail being used as part of a hoist. *B.Bourne.*

The back of the building, at the side of what in 1903 was the smithy. Inside the door to the right is the last gas lamp. *B.Bourne.*

Outside the Engine Shed in 1965, the turntable is intact, but the site is overgrown. *Alf Henshaw.*

Taken from outside the Coaling Stage Tank House in 1965, this photograph shows weeds growing between the rails. Note the Uttoxeter Old Road bridge in the background. *Alf Henshaw.*

Inside the shed in 1996. Note the original metal support and the supporting arch. *B.Bourne.*

The back of the building in 1996, showing where there was another building attached to the back. The small building at the back was a smithy. There is a doorway with stairs that was workers' access to Slack Lane. Just inside this doorway is the last remaining gas lamp, still in place after all these years. *B.Bourne.*

The last remaining gas lamp still in its original position, in what was once the passageway with stairs that led up to Slack Lane. *S.Bourne.*

A view towards the Engine Shed. To the right note the brick platform which has a large wooden joist running along the top. Note how new brickwork has been added and the whole thing built up, although the shape of the original steps can still be seen. According to the plans for the station, it can only be the platform to the Coaling Stage Tank House. Today, it has been extended back across where the Tank House stood and has been turned into a weighbridge. *S.Bourne.*

The former Macmillan's printers in 1996 and to the right what was Evans' Mineral Water Factory. *B.Bourne.*

Chimney behind Macmillan's, close to the Cement Store. *B.Bourne.*

Behind Macmillans is this odd building which can only be the Cement Store, very overgrown and unsafe. This photograph taken from the front shows the building to be mainly made of corrugated iron. *B.Bourne.*

A view of the Cement Store taken from the back. You can see a canopy. In the undergrowth are signs of where the tracks ran. *B.Bourne.*

The Cement Store showing the canopy partially collapsed and wooden running boards that acted as the platform but when this photograph was taken in 1996 were just rotting away. *B.Bourne.*

This wooden door, on the side of the building on the opposite side to the platform, was possibly used as a goods entrance. *B.Bourne.*

This is the view walking from behind the Cement Stores, showing the bridge from Slack Lane to the firms across the tracks. Originally Coles' Crane Works and Bennetts' brickfield, and later part of Hazelwoods. At the front of the bridge was Jones' Tan Works. All these had their own sidings. *B.Bourne.*

Viewed from the other side (to the previous photograph), which is now a park. The bridge now backs on to the Kingsway commercial development. *B.Bourne.*

The bridge from Slack Lane over the tracks to what was, according to the plans of 1880, Coles' Crane Works and Bennetts' brickfield. *B.Bourne.*

Part of the buildings on Slack Lane, alongside the tracks, that formed Jones' Tan Works.

Jack Wallis, who was a driver in the 1950s, told me that dog manure was used in the tanning process!

The building was taken over in the 1950s by Burrrows & Sturgess, who made soft drinks and used their own siding until the mid 1960s. Apparently few alterations were made to the premises. In a loft, some 2,000 pith helmets from around the Boer War period were discovered. These were given to the local children and at one time every child in the district must have been running round in one. *B.Bourne.*

A view from the bridge from Slack Lane to where Hazelwood foods had their head office in 1996. The company's premises later extended over where the tracks ran. In the 1950s and 1960s this was Pelapone Ltd who made glass bottles. *S.Bourne.*

Looking up towards Bramble Brook. From here the line went to Stafford. *S.Bourne.*

Well Street in 1996, looking down to Bath Street. To the left would have been part of Handyside's Sidings, Handyside is famous for the railway bridges over Friargate and the Derwent. The company also made the roofs at London's Broad Street Station and Manchester Central Station, the Barton swing-aqueduct across the Manchester Ship Canal, and also many steel-framed buildings including the Savoy Hotel in London. In this photograph St Alkmund's Well is at the bottom left, just behind the bushes. Today it is basically just a hole in the ground with a few steps. An attempt has been made to gentrify it with a few benches, but it is tucked away in this quiet street and almost forgotten. In the background are the only high-rise flats in Derby. *S.Bourne.*

The Furnace pub in Duke Street was built to serve the rail workers and men from the many firms in the area. Originally it was only licensed to sell ale. The siding to C.W.T. Wheeldon's ran very close to the pub, roughly where the slab path is on the right. There was also a buffer stop just outside the pub, and a crane and weighbridge close by. Looking at Duke Street today, it is hard to imagine that this was a busy Goods Yard with sidings for Handyside's, C.W.T. Wheeldon's (formally Shaw's Mill) and George Holme & Co.

Handyside's went bankrupt in 1910, 1923 and again in 1931. It then became Derby Castings but eventually folded in 1933. The demise of Duke Street took place as the firms it had been built to serve either went bankrupt, felt they would be better served by road not rail, or moved altogether. *B.Bourne.*

Bath Street Mills in 1996, owned by a Mr Butler who lives in Ashbourne. He has owned the building since 1958 and has let it to various firms in that time. It is actually two mills. At the rear, Derby Cotton had it for a time before closing around 1950. To start with the mills were owned by a silk, woollen and elastic fabrics manufacturer but they went out of business by the 1920s. Mr Butler also told me that the mill was built around 1890 and that after the elastic firm left, a shoe manufacturer called Maden & Ireland took over. In 1913, when George Holme & Co had the building, it did have its own siding. At one time, Mr Butler told me, as many as ten firms were using it at the same time. The mill is now occupied mostly by Trio, a firm of contract upholsterers. Mr Neil King told me they have been there for around 25 years. Inside the building has undergone some changes as different firms have occupied it, but the owner makes sure it is well maintained as an interesting example of industrial architecture. *J.Coker.*

View walking along from Duke Street. The building was Bath Street Mills, one of the few remaining on the Duke Street site where new houses and flats have been built. Duke Street closed to goods traffic in 1948, but was still used for a time. There was a Parcel Transfer Shed and a Goods Depot. Browns' Mills used the sidings, as did Chadwick & Lunts and other small firms. *B.Bourne.*

Jack Wallis told me that when he lived in Handyside Street (which was built on Handyside's factory site) his neighbour was digging a hole for an air-raid shelter during the war, when he dug up a boiler and railway lines which he sold for scrap. *B.Bourne.*

The only reminder of the Handyside foundry. This street was built on the site and nothing remains today. A lot of things were buried on the site, so one imagines that the gardens could yield some very interesting finds. *J.Coker.*

The side of what was Bath Street Mills, now occupied by Trio, the upholsters. I was kindly shown round by Matt Flowers. There are still some air-raid shelters at the rear, now filled with rubble. Running alongside this outside wall was the mills' own siding, which was still there in 1913. *S.Bourne.*

Behind the wall was the Darley Grove headshunt, which ran from the Excursion Platform on Friargate Station right into Darley Park. *B.Bourne.*

Old metal fencing and a small gate lead to some hard standing. Embedded in the concrete are bits of what look like metal posts. There could have been a building here, or signals. To the left, the line of the tracks can be seen. *B.Bourne.*

Handyside's bridge over the River Derwent. To the left can be seen the beginning of the tunnel which carried the Duke Street Sidings under the main line from Friargate. *B.Bourne.*

The narrow tunnel under the main line. The line of the tracks can now be seen as a footpath. *B.Bourne.*

The GNR's bridge across the River Derwent in 1963. This bridge was built at the request of the Town Council and was to include a public footpath from Little Chester to North Parade. *Ken Cook.*

A similar view taken in 1974. *Ken Cook.*

LNER 2-8-0 No 6174 passing Breadsall in the 1950s.
Alan Rimmer.

It is very hard to see the number but this could be 44067, on Derby Friargate in 1964.
Alf Bousie.

This photograph was taken near Derby Racecourse Sidings in 1965. Alf Henshaw and his brother almost got thrown off the site for trespassing, but were kindly allowed to continue taking pictures by officials. Most of the photographs taken by Alf Henshaw were used by his brother for model making.

Four photographs of Bennerley Viaduct, between Awsworth and Ilkeston, which was constructed for the GNR in 1878 by Richard Johnson. It is one of only two remaining all-metal viaducts, the other being Meldon Viaduct at Okehampton. It closed to passenger traffic in 1964, remaining operational to freight until 1968. It is 500 yards wide and 60ft high and is a Grade II listed building. About five years ago it had some restoration to its northern end where it crosses an operational line. *B.Bourne.*

Memorabilia

IN this final small chapter are a few interesting pieces I have come across in my travels, all from private collections. Scrap trains would collect all the signs and notices, and anything else that hadn't already been 'liberated', from all the closed-down stations. These would end up at St Andrew's Goods Warehouse, near Midland Road, to be sold off. During the 1960s Friargate memorabilia came up often. Now it is very rare, and what is left is treasured by its owners. Of course, I have only seen a very small selection. For instance, where did all the lamps go? I suspect a lot were melted down for scrap but a few, I'm sure, a garden or two.

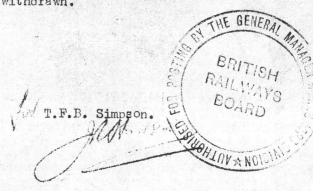

```
                                        S6/3

   British Railways Workshops,              SDL.25
   Loco. Works Manager's Office,
   DERBY.                                   29th July, 1964


                        N O T I C E


              RE-SHAPING OF THE RAILWAYS: PASSENGER
                            CLOSURES


         I have been advised by the Line Manager, Derby, that as from
   7th September, 1964, the passenger train service between Nottingham
   Victoria and Derby Friargate will be withdrawn.




                              T.F.B. Simpson.
```

Notice given to BR workers telling them of the imminent closure of Friargate. *Ken Cook.*

```
THE LAST PUBLIC SERVICE PASSENGER TRAIN ON
THE RAILWAY LINE FROM NOTTINGHAM VICTORIA to
DERBY FRIARGATE

Date: 5/9/64
Time: 22.30  ex.Nottingham Vic.
Loco: 2-6-0  ex M&GN.(LMS) Ivatt No. 43058
Driver: 'Barlow' (Colwick)
Stock: 6 BR. Suburban Coaches.
```

Station.	Sch.	Arr.	Dep.	Passengers On.	Off.
NOTTINGHAM Victoria	:22.30	-	22.31	130.	-
New BASFORD	-	-	-	-	-
BASFORD N.	22.39	-	22.39	2	10
KIMBERLEY	22.43	22.47	22.49	unknown	(Crowds)
AWSWORTH	22.47	22.50	22.52	5	1
ILKESTON	22.51	22.54	22.58	5	15
W.HALLAM	-	-	-	-	-
DERBY Friargate:	23.05	23.10	-	-	All.

```
Amen.
```

Ken Cook made this record of the last train journey from Friargate. He lists everything from the driver to the passengers and, of course, kept his ticket. Some people had their tickets signed by the driver and porters.

A selection of
tickets from
Friargate
including a period
parking ticket
which allowed
the driver to park
his vehicle under
the arches.

A Guard's lamp
from Friargate.

Sadly, this is all that is left of the Derby East Signal Box, apart from a pile of rubble.

It is believed that this sign is from the Coaling Stage Tank House.

This sign was situated outside what is now the Cob Shop on Friargate.

One of the station signs from the platform.

Above and right: signs from the Goods Depot.